IMAGES
of England

PLYMOUTH ARGYLE
FOOTBALL CLUB
1886-1986

IMAGES
of England

PLYMOUTH ARGYLE
FOOTBALL CLUB
1886-1986

Compiled by
Gordon Sparks

TEMPUS

First published 1998
Copyright © Gordon Sparks, 1998

Tempus Publishing Limited
The Mill, Brimscombe Port,
Stroud, Gloucestershire, GL5 2QG

ISBN 0 7524 1185 3

Typesetting and origination by
Tempus Publishing Limited
Printed in Great Britain by
Midway Clark Printing, Wiltshire

Present and forthcoming football titles from Tempus Publishing:

Bristol Rovers Football Club 1986-1996
Burnley Football Club
Bury Football Club
Cardiff City Football Club 1899-1947
Cardiff City Football Club 1947-1971
Charlton Athletic Football Club
Crystal Palace Football Club
Exeter City Football Club 1904-1994
Gillingham Football Club
Newport County Football Club 1912-1960
Oxford United Football Club
Plymouth Argyle Football Club 1886-1986
Reading Football Club 1871-1997
Sheffield United Football Club
Sunderland Football Club
Swansea Town Football Club 1912-64
Tranmere Rovers Football Club
West Ham United Football Club
Wrexham Football Club
York City Football Club

Contents

Sam Rendell is generally regarded as Mr Plymouth Argyle. A modest man, Sam has supported his local side all his life and deservedly holds the title of President of Plymouth Argyle Football Club. His many decades of active involvement in life at Home Park continues on the most personal level possible, illustrated perfectly on each match day, when supporters and guests are given guided tours of the stadium with a full verbal history of The Pilgrims. Sam also regularly receives parties of schoolchildren and, in doing so, does his best to guarantee a healthy fan base amongst future generations. Every football club, no matter how big or small, should have its own Sam Rendell.

Foreword

It is indeed a compliment to be invited to prepare the foreword to an account of the history of Plymouth Argyle Football Club compiled by such an enthusiastic supporter as Gordon Sparks. By his writings and on his programmes for local radio, Gordon has been tireless in his efforts to promote the best interests of the club. We are indebted to him for the time spent in research for the preparation of this illustration of the club's first 100 years.

It is readily appreciated that our first consideration must ever be the future of the club – its success and progress in the years ahead are of vital importance. However, a great deal of pleasure is felt and a measure of pride experienced when considering events of the past. There have also been times of anxiety and stress for the club and its supporters. During the two World Wars, Plymouth Argyle ceased to operate: indeed, in 1941, during an air attack on the city, Home Park was severely damaged and the fine grandstand, built just eleven years earlier on the occasion of the club's promotion for the first time from Division Three (South) to Division Two, was destroyed.

A tribute must be paid to directors, managers, players, administrative staff, ground staff and all those who have served the club so faithfully over the years, not to mention the generations of supporters who have continued to support the club so loyally in times good and not so good.

So much has happened since, after having been an amateur organisation for seventeen years, the club embraced professionalism in 1903. Then, our local support was from the three towns of Plymouth, Stonehouse and Devonport and followers made their way to Home Park on foot or by electric tramcar. Supporters from surrounding localities would travel by train and local stations would be very busy on match days. Home Park itself, where the club first played in 1901, was a truly rural area, the ground being surrounded by fields in which horses and cattle from the nearby farm would be grazing.

I would like to take this opportunity to quote just a few verses from a poem by Albert Webb, which appeared regularly in the club handbooks prior to the First World War.

Five years ago, the Argyle launch'd
Their ship on stormy sea;
The good old craft still bravely floats,
Her flag flies merrily.

Their motto ever famous
The good old 'One and All';
One aim, one voice, one will,
For success with the ball.

The crowds will see and crowds will cheer
And points be notched each week;
The football world will echo far,
Argyle is hard to beat.

Let each one's aim be unison,
Work all your very best;
Then rest assured, the championship,
Will come then to the West.

The five years in the opening line have extended to over a century, but the sentiments remain unchanged as we look to the future and we wish Plymouth Argyle Football Club all the success and good fortune it merits.

Sam Rendell
1998

Acknowledgements

I am proud to have supported Plymouth Argyle since the age of five, a following that I have been fortunate enough to carry on through my career in broadcasting and writing. I am proud because, as a Plymothian, I have not been lured into following 'bigger' clubs from a distance but stayed loyal to my club – which has rewarded me with many, although sporadic, memorable occasions. To follow the fortunes of Plymouth Argyle has brought its disappointments, but along the way there have always been characters and events with colourful stories to tell.

I hope this collection of photographs, memorabilia and archive material serves as an item of reminiscence for other long-standing supporters and as a source of education for those who have a lifetime of green blood yet to flow through their veins.

I am very grateful to all those people who have supplied photographs from their collections to supplement the items from my own. To Sam Rendell, the President of Plymouth Argyle, who is nothing short of a walking encyclopaedia of knowledge; Colin Parsons, whose generosity in allowing the inclusion of some of the rarest items ever to be seen has been hugely appreciated; Dave Rowntree, the photographer who has braved snow, driving rain and heatwaves in the pursuit of excellent coverage, and also Paul Truscott and Phil Hollow, two members of the Plymouth Argyle Programme Collectors' Club who have collated items concerning matters that few modern Argyle fans are aware of. I would also like to thank Peter Hall, the jovial former office manager, who in his retirement is now doing much for the future of the game with his involvement in youth football. Thank you, gentlemen all.

Thanks must also go to Tempus Publishing, particularly James (who has a soft spot for The 'Gyles), for the opportunity to put another Plymouth Argyle title on the supporters' bookshelves. Last, but by no means least, I am grateful to Plymouth Argyle Football Club for the use of official club photographs – may we soon see you back where you belong.

I would like to finish with a special thanks to my wife, Heather, for her patience and support.

Introduction

It can hardly be said that Plymouth Argyle has been one of the great names in British football. They have yet to appear in the highest echelon of the League, yet to grace a major cup final at Wembley Stadium (although there have been near misses) and yet to be mispronounced by European journalists. Many would argue that the glorious times for a club formed in 1886, albeit in a town passionate about rugby rather than football, should by now have arrived.

But, as the years have rolled by, there have been many famous names involved with Plymouth Argyle, both on and off the field. The first of those, Frank Brettell, led the side into the Southern League. Robert Jack then went on to lead the side into the Football League and beyond, in a protracted term of management that is unheard of in the modern climate of huge wages and short contracts. There have been great players such as Sammy Black, 'Jumbo' Chisholm and Paul Mariner. Men such as these have raised the expectations of fans starved of major success: the good folk of Plymouth, the surrounding areas, and those in exile who still travel thousands of miles each season to see their team.

This book charts the progress of the first hundred years of the club described by many, for so long, as 'The Sleeping Giant'. There are many rare items included, some of which have never before been published, which help trace the history of The Pilgrims – still sailing in search of the Promised Land…

A great man, not only to Plymouth Argyle Football Club but Plymouth as a whole, A.C. Ballard became the chairman of the football club in the city that he loved. His shrewd business brain was never at ease within the confines of Home Park. In 1933, he attempted to pioneer a new move to assist the players, as he became the first chairman of a Football League club to offer an aeroplane for journeys to away matches. Unfortunately, the Football League management committee did not consider the suggestion worthy of adoption. Mr Ballard even went as far as making a trial run, albeit to no avail, arriving at Stoke City's ground after two-and-a-quarter hours of travelling while the players spent eight hours on a train. Surely, A.C. Ballard was a man ahead of his time.

One
The Dawn of
a New Club

One of the earliest team photos, with various attires on show. From left to right, back row: Thomas Floyd (Hon. Secretary), F. Crouch (Hon. Secretary), E. Duncalf, P. Buchan (Captain), A. Ledington, W. Nicol, Clarence Spooner (President). Middle row: C. Peters, C. Hovey, C. Pethick, F. Derry. Front row: S. Vosper, R. Holmes, H. Rose, R. Dann, D. Pascho.

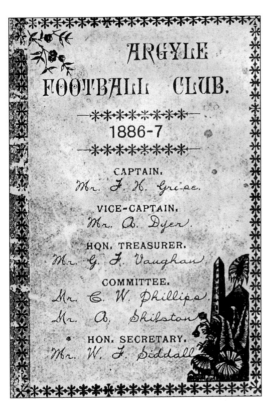

ARGYLE FOOTBALL CLUB.

✳✳✳✳✳✳✳✳
1886-7
✳✳✳✳✳✳✳✳

CAPTAIN.
Mr. F. H. Grose.

VICE-CAPTAIN.
Mr. A. Dyer.

HON. TREASURER.
Mr. G. F. Vaughan

COMMITTEE.
Mr. C. W. Phillips
Mr. A. Shilston

HON. SECRETARY.
Mr. W. F. Siddall

The official fixture card from Plymouth Argyle's first competitive season. The sports ground of Dunheved College provided the venue against, appropriately, one of the colleges whose former pupils played a major role in the formation of the team – including captain F.H. Grose and W. Pethybridge, who travelled to Plymouth from Launceston to take up employment.

ARGYLE FOOTBALL [CLU]B. ✳✳✳ Fixtures 1886-7.

DATE.	AGAINST.	WHERE PLAYED.	RESULT.	
			FOR.	AGAINS[T]
Oct. 9	Dunheved College............	Launceston	0	2
— 30	Plymouth College	College Ground	2	1
Nov. 6	Royal Artillery	Granby................		
— 13	Tavistock Grammar School	Tavistock		
— 20	Mannamead School............	Hartley................		
Dec. 4	Hotspur	Beaconsfield		
— 11	Plymouth United............	Beaconsfield		
Jan. 22	Mannamead School *Return*.	Hartley......		
Feb. 5	Hotspur *Return*............	Beaconsfield		
— 19	Corporation Grammar School	Lilley......		
Mar. 5	Plymouth United *Return*......	Beaconsfield............		
— 12	Plymouth College *Return*	College Ground		

12

Argyle Football Club.

SEASON 1898-99.

President:
CLARE. CE.SPOONER, Esq.

Vice=Presidents:

C. E. BOOLDS, Esq	G. P. FISHER, Esq.
E. H. BABB, Esq.	HOWARD GROSE, Esq.
C. E. BRITTAN, Esq.	H. HOLDSTOCK, Esq.
G. BLIGHT, Esq.	V. J. PROUT, Esq.
W. CORNISH, Esq.	B. PARKHOUSE, Esq.

A. H. SHILSTON, Esq.

Patrons:

F. CROUCH, Esq.	T. ROWSE, Esq.
R. HARVEY DAW, Esq	A. V. R OKE, Esq
T. W. GINN, Esq.	W. BISHOP, Esq.

G. N TTING, Esq.

Club Ground . . . . MARSH MILLS.
(The Club runs a Special Train.)

Colours . . . . GREEN AND BLACK.

OFFICERS.

	1st Eleven.	Reserves.
Captain	E. J. DILLON	A. CROUCH.
Vice=Captain	A. P. FISHER	S. G. L. PHILP.

Hon. Secretary and Treasurer WM. ROWSE, 1, Montrose Terrace, Houndiscor e Road.

Committee: MARTIN R. OZ R. C. FLOYD.
C. H HOSKIN. E. A. HODGE.
F. C W LLOUGHBY.

Under new Club President, Clarence Spooner, a club rulebook was published. It is interesting to note, from the front cover, that the home ground was listed as Marsh Mills on the outskirts of Plymouth, which could be reached by the townspeople via specially chartered trains. Rules eleven and twelve were strictly enforced, meriting their inclusion in bold typeface.

RULES.

1. That the Club be called the "Argyle Football Club."

2. That the Colours of the Club be Green and Black, and every Member appear in such when playing for the Club. Any Member transgressing this rule will pay the County fine.

3. That before any person is admitted a Member of the Club he shall be elected by the Committee, his name and address to be given to the Secretary.

4. That the Annual Subscription for Members be 5s., payable on or before October 1st in every year.

5. That the Annual General Meeting be held during the first week in June, and that at least seven days' notice be sent to each Member.

6. The Officers of the Club shall consist of a Captain and Vice-Captain for each team, a Treasurer, Secretary, and Committee, who shall be elected each year at the Annual Meeting.

7. That the Committee consist of ten Members, of whom the Captains, Vice-Captains, Treasurer, and Secretary shall be *ex-officio* Members, and that four constitute a quorum.

8. That the Captain or Vice-Captain of each team shall submit his eleven each week for the approval of the Committee.

9. That any Member promising to play in a match and being subsequently unable to do so, must give his Captain at least twenty-four hours' notice, or a fine of 2s. 6d. will be enforced. Any Member transgressing this rule shall be dealt with as the Committee think proper.

10. That in case of any question arising as to these Rules, the same may be referred to the Committee, whose decision shall be final.

11. Any playing Member smoking within four hours prior to a match will be fined 1s.

12. "Kicking about" prior to a match is forbidden.

13

PROGRAMME.
Home Park, November 15th, 1902.

	WEST BROMWICH ALBION.	

			GOAL.			
			Taylor			
			BACKS.			
	Chadburn				Jones	
			HALF-BACKS.			
Gollings		Appleby			Randle	
			FORWARDS.			
A. Smith			Hobson			E. Smith
Fern						Harper
Right.		*Centre.*			*Left.*	

REFEREE ◯ MR. S. W. CARTER, o.r.

Left.		*Centre.*			*Right.*
		FORWARDS.			
Andrews			Sylvester		Wheaton
J. Matters					Scarr
		HALF-BACKS.			
Matters		Pethick			Broad
		BACKS.			
Wyatt				Hare	
		GOAL.			
		Buchan			

ARGYLE.

LOOK OUT FOR ARGYLE RUGBY v. PAIGNTON, WEDNESDAY NEXT, AT 3-15. (left column)

LOOK OUT FOR ARGYLE RUGBY v. PAIGNTON, WEDNESDAY NEXT, AT 3-15. (right column)

Adlard Bros., Printers, Plymouth.

Many people held the pessimistic view that a professional football team in Plymouth would be nothing more than a passing phase, but there was a great deal of interest shown in the exhibition matches held during 1902. West Bromwich Albion helped to fuel local enthusiasm and, as this single-sheet programme shows, courtesy was not forgotten as the visitors were listed above the hosts.

The need to appoint a well-educated man at the helm was fulfilled when Irishman Frank Brettell took charge of the team. Brettell had twenty-eight years' experience of top-class football administration behind him, having been secretary of Everton, from the club's inception in 1875, and, ten years later, joining Bolton Wanderers in the same capacity. In 1896, he had moved south and set Spurs on their way into the Southern League before advising Portsmouth in similar circumstances two years later. His personal success story continued with Argyle.

Two
Southern League Days

Under Brettell, Plymouth Argyle was granted acceptance to compete in The Southern League for the 1903/04 season. From left to right, standing: Wattie Anderson, H. Winterhalder, Charlie Clark, Jack Fitchett, Jack Robinson, Andy Clark, J. Banks, Jack Picken, Robert Jack. Seated: T. Cleghorn, Bob Dalrymple, Billy Leech, Archie Goodall, Jack Peddie, Harry Digweed, Frank Brettell (Manager).

The ~~Hon: Sec:~~ Chairman & Hon Sec. reported that they had had an interview with Lieut Windrum & Mr. Clarence Spooner the Chairman & a Director of the proposed Plymouth Argyle F.C. Ltd who were desirous of entering this League if they could also gain admission to the Southern League. With a view to the matter being fully discussed at the next meeting the following particulars were given :—

Capital £3000, £1700 already guaranteed voluntarily by friends of Promoters. the whole practically applied for now. Directors are also prepared to put in extra money themselves if necessary

Ground fully equipped — Dressing rooms for 5 teams with Hot & cold Baths &c.
Stand accomodation for 2000, only expense on ground 3 further Turnstiles. Lease about 12½ years @ £100 a year. Trams from all parts pass

Team will be absolutely the best they can obtain, will spend practically the whole of their Capital in securing class men, will not touch players of clubs in Southern or Western Leagues. Team manager will be a first class man, have practically engaged him. He is a well known man

Excerpt from the Western League minute book of the details concerning Plymouth Argyle's application to join the Western League. The same squad of players also played in the Southern

Matches Midweek on Wednesdays.

Train service is excellent London served by
G.W.R. & L.+S.W.R.

Directors are all prominent Plymouth men &
men of means.

Rugby opposition is very strong & the promoters
of the new club will use every endeavour
to gain a large share of the patronage of
the Football public. A large number of
the Dockyard hands are Association
followers but have now only junior teams
to watch so patronise Rugby matches.

The Members were asked to consider the
matter & discuss it with their Directorates &
the whole question to be further gone into at the
next meeting of the Committee.

The following Referees were appointed for March.
Mon. 2nd Brentford v West Ham.   J Harrower.
  "   9th   "   v Tottenham.   A. Millward   Kick
  "   .   West Ham v Millwall .   A.G. Arkell.   off
Wed. 11th Portsmouth v Queen's P.R. J.C. Tillotson 3.30
Mon 16th West Ham v Brentford .   H.D. Casey.   p.m.
  " 23rd Southampton v Bristol Rovers. F. Crabtree – 3.45
Confirmed

                                    R. Riddell
                            12th March 1903.

League. It is interesting to note the capital required, details of the ground, descriptions of players, manager and directors, and the efforts made to sway the Plymouth public towards football in a rugby stronghold.

Half back Charlie Clark, made his Plymouth Argyle debut in the third match of the inaugural Southern League season. Over the next seven years, he played in 183 Southern League, 17 FA Cup and 73 Western League games. Even more notable than this impressive record is the fact that he became the first professional captain of the club.

The results from the first season of Southern League and Western League participation, accompanied by the FA Cup scores that saw Argyle progress through four qualifying ties to meet Sheffield Wednesday in the First Round.

SOUTHERN LEAGUE.

DATE.	OPPONENTS.	Ground.	For.	Agst.
1903.				
Sept. 5	Northampton	Home	2	0
„ 12	Brentford	Away	0	1
„ 19	West Ham United	Home	2	0
„ 26	Tottenham Hotspurs ...	Away	2	0
Oct. 3	Luton	Home	0	0
„ 10	New Brompton	Away	0	0
„ 17	Kettering	Home	5	1
„ 24	Southampton	Away	5	3
Nov. 7	Millwall	Away	0	1
„ 11	Fulham	Home	1	0
„ 21	Swindon	Away	0	2
Dec. 5	Wellingborough	Home	4	1
„ 19	Brighton and Hove Albion	Home	4	2
„ 25	Reading	Home	0	1
„ 26	Bristol Rovers	Away	2	1
„ 28	Portsmouth	Away	0	0
1904.				
Jan. 2	Northampton	Away	0	1
„ 9	Brentford	Home	2	2
„ 16	West Ham United ...	Away	1	1
„ 23	Tottenham Hotspurs ...	Home	1	3
„ 30	Luton	Away	1	1
Feb. 13	Kettering	Away	0	3
„ 20	Brighton and Hove Albion ...	Away	0	0
„ 27	Fulham	Away	0	1
Mar. 5	Millwall	Home	2	3
„ 9	Southampton	Home	0	2
„ 12	Queen's Park Rangers ...	Away	0	1
„ 16	New Brompton	Home	1	0
„ 19	Swindon	Home	0	0
Apr. 1	Bristol Rovers	Home	0	0
„ 2	Wellingborough	Away	3	1
„ 4	Reading	Away	3	1
„ 13	Queen's Park Rangers ...	Home	1	1
„ 23	Portsmouth	Home	2	0

WESTERN LEAGUE.

DATE.	OPPONENTS.	Ground.	For.	Agst.
1903.				
Sept. 1	West Ham United	Away	1	0
„ 9	Portsmouth	Away	2	1
„ 14	Queen's Park Rangers ...	Away	1	1
„ 30	Portsmouth	Home	3	1
Oct. 12	Bristol Rovers	Away	0	3
Nov. 18	Southampton	Home	2	0
1904.				
Jan. 4	Southampton	Away	2	1
Feb. 24	Queen's Park Rangers ...	Home	0	1
„ 29	Tottenham Hotspurs ...	Away	1	5
Mar. 23	Brentford	Home	0	0
„ 26	Reading	Away	1	2
Apr. 5	Brentford	Away	1	0
„ 9	Bristol Rovers	Home	2	2
„ 20	Tottenham Hotspurs ...	Home	0	0
„ 27	West Ham	Home	3	2
„ 30	Reading	Home	4	0

ENGLISH CUP ROUNDS.

DATE.	OPPONENTS.	Ground.	For.	Agst.
Oct. 31	Whiteheads	Home	7	0
Nov. 14	Freemantle	Home	5	1
„ 28	Swindon	Home	2	0
Dec. 12	Brentford	Away	1	1
„ 16	„ (replayed) ...	Home	4	1
Feb. 6	Sheffield Wednesday ...	Home	2	2
„ 10	„ „ (replayed)	Away	0	2

Argyle won the 1904/05 Western League Championship. This picture is taken from the 4-1 win over Southampton on 28 September, with The Saints preparing to take a throw in. The supporters that can be seen on the far side of the ground are occupying the position of today's Popular Stand.

Reporting on the fortunes of a football club brings the responsibility of fully describing the action of each match. With the pen name of 'The Traveller', H.J. Long began his writing love affair with Plymouth Argyle in 1905 and served readers of *The Evening Herald* and *The Football Herald* for more than a quarter of a century.

Described as one of the finest goalkeepers England has ever produced, Yorkshireman John Willie Sutcliffe has the distinction of being the only player to gain international honours in both rugby (1899) and association codes. He was famous for his performance in the 1894 Cup Final, despite being on the Bolton Wanderers side that lost 4-1 to Notts County in front of 37,000 spectators at Goodison Park. Sutcliffe was not in his youth when he arrived at Home Park in 1905 for Southern League football, but displayed a lot of class in his 172 matches over seven years.

Having played local football with Green Waves and represented Devon County, Plymouth-born Billy Baker gained experience in the United States and South Africa before playing for Argyle. A plucky player, often described as a 'pocket Hercules', the left half had a strong personality that made him a popular member of the team. It took him four years to break into the first team and, from 1909, ensure that Robert Jack selected him as an automatic choice. Baker made 193 appearances before the First World War put paid to Southern League football and his career with The Greens. Alas, Baker was killed during the war.

In the first Southern League season, Plymothian W.H. 'Tich' Horne made his debut on 30 January 1903 in the 1-1 draw at Luton. He had to be a patient man as, despite regular attention from other clubs, he remained the reserve team goalkeeper until 1911. He was permitted, however, to play with Fulham on loan. Regular games for Argyle eventually came his way and he had made 197 Southern League appearances by the time he departed from the club in December 1914. Perhaps his loyalty to his home club was a result of the time he spent in the Duke of Cornwall's Regiment, with whom he served in the South African campaign.

Fred Craig scored five goals for Argyle – not a bad tally for a goalkeeper! The goals were all penalties. Those who witnessed his arrival from Larkhill Thistle, a previously unheard of junior club in Lancashire, in 1912, would not have believed that he would be the regular 'keeper until 1930. His impressive attendance record would have been even greater had it not been for the First World War. His seventy-eight Southern League games ended with League status. The first of his 361 games in the Football League was the historic opening match of the 1921/22 season, a 3-1 win at Bristol Rovers. His final match came in the promotion season that, at last, elevated the club into Division Two. The Scotsman, who also captained Argyle, was selected for an Anglo-Scots XI in 1917. He still had much to offer on leaving Plymouth, as the supporters of his next club, Barrow, were to discover: the club was bottom of Division Three (North) on his arrival but that was soon to change.

Left back Septimus Atterbury arrived in 1907, a seventeen year-old from Southern League rivals Swindon Town. He became a loyal servant to Plymouth Argyle, tasting success both on and off the field. He appeared in a green shirt for 261 Southern League matches – culminating in the achievement of Football League status – before playing thirty matches in the club's first Division Three (South) season. Atterbury became a trainer in 1921, the year in which a benefit match against his former club was played in front of 7,000 spectators. His backroom influence helped Argyle to the Division Three (South) Championship in 1930.

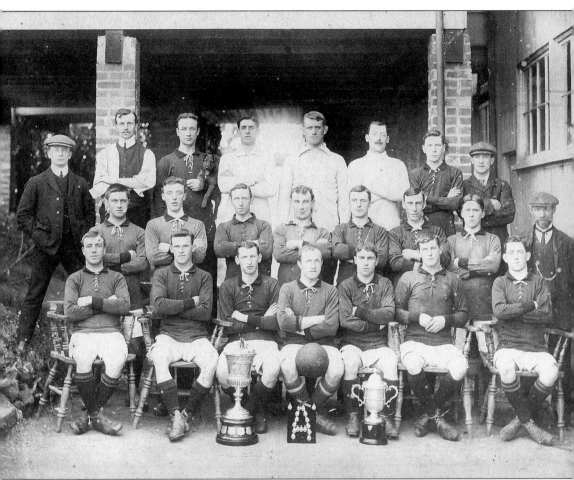

This very rare photograph shows the Plymouth Argyle Reserves team of the 1907/08 season, proudly displaying the Devon County Senior Cup and Plymouth and District League Cup. Pictured behind the original stand at Home Park, from left to right, back row: Louis H. Crabb (Team Secretary), N. Wallis (Trainer), F.W. Black, A.E. Moore, W. 'Tich' Horne, G. Sandy, V. Worden, G.H. Whitefield. Middle row: J. Ellery, W. Giles, H. Ridler, Billy Baker, J. Cudlipp, J. Simmons, A. Tucker, W. Tomlinson (Groundsman). Front row: T. Haynes, A. Peard, F. Burch, A.J. Wheaton (Captain), J. Meager, S. Tozer, H. Leavey.

Robert Jack became the first player to sign professional terms with the club on his arrival from Bolton Wanderers in 1903. He succeeded his former manager, Frank Brettell, in 1905, whilst remaining in the Argyle side. A year later he left for Southend. However, in 1910, Jack returned to Home Park and managed the side for an incredible twenty-eight years. Robert Jack's sons, David and Rollo, both played for Argyle in the 1920s. Another son, Donald, played reserve team football for the club before following in his father's footsteps and playing League football for Bolton Wanderers (as did David and Rollo in later years).

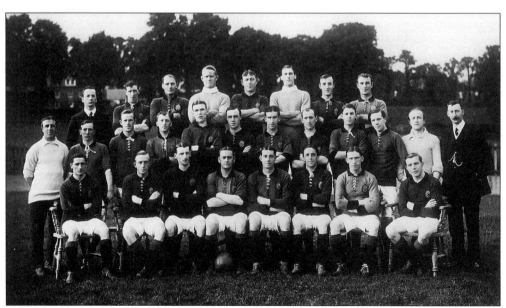

With their splendidly groomed hair, the squad is assembled and ready for the start of the 1912/13 campaign.

Reminiscences and Ruminations.

OUR EASTERTIDE VISITORS—and some old-time happenings.

"POMPEY" AND "THE PILGRIMS."

OUR visitors this holiday season, appropriately enough, themselves smack of holidays, although all will agree that the holidays that they remind us of are not those spent beside the fire with a blanket around one's shoulders, a warming pan under our feet, and a little tot of something hot on the mantel-piece. Mind you, I am not guaranteeing that such are our present conditions. But certainly, as I write early in the week, such would appear to be our lot this Eastertide. Not so bad either, these conditions. It depends very much on the size of the glass on the mantelpiece, does'nt it? But Pompey and Plymouth remind us of a warmer time, even, when we stroll around the South Coast as though we were the ground landlords and had been there fcr years, forgetting that each little girl in a South Coast town knows each little boy, and blissfully ignorant of the fact that such little girls have already marked us down as foreign goods. Yes, they bring with them the balmy breezes of the Downs and the Moor, and as we murmur, "Well played, Portsmouth" or "Buck up, the Pilgrims," we can feel upon our cheeks more salt air and crisp ozone than ever gathered upon the main sail of a Thames mud barge. The Weary Winds of the West—I wonder what they are blowing unto us to-day! They begin upon the writer by clearing some of the cobwebs that old Time has allowed to gather in his knowledge box, and methinks I am down at old Fratton hearing the crowd, composed of four parts military and two parts civilian and naval boys, yell their advice, free gratis and for nothing, at the players of the 15th Coy. R.G.A., who once disported themselves for their own benefit and the edification of the Portsmouth public in the Army, Hampshire and English Cups.

The old R.A.

You all remember "Ginger" Reilly! Of course you do. Well known to Londoners was "Ginger," after a time. But some of us knew him long before he thought of coming to the Metropolis. A fine goalkeeper and a great Portsmouth favourite. Then there was Sergeants Phillips and Hanna, and Jardine, all really good players. The gentlemen who set about getting a class team together for this Company knew a thing or two about football, I can tell you. But they touched closer home than the above would have us suppose. Do you remember Jimmy Meggs! No! Well, let me tell you that Jimmy Meggs was one of the finest forwards who never rose to greatness. Many a time and oft has he spelt downfall to Millwall and other London clubs. He was an old St. Paul boy, and as a member of Old St. Paul's he set London afire. He could run like a very deer, dribble with a close ball always under control, and shoot—mind you, shoot—from outside right as hot as many an inside man *attempts* to nowadays. I have seen him drive a ball just under the bar from the touch line at such a pace that the goalie's hands have been knocked back in his attempt to clear. Of course, Jimmy could'nt stay with St. Paul's with football in London developing as it then was, and, again of course, he soon found himself with our friends the dear old enemy at Woolwich. There he did great execution and provided them with their missing link. From being an ordinary amateur team they became a really great one—such a one

indeed that no London club could stand against them. And Jimmy Meggs had a lion's share in making them. What a hot headed fellow he was! Originally intended, I believe, for a schoolmaster, he spent most of his time footballing and boxing—and my word, he could use them, could Jimmy. And after all he enlisted, and blossomed as the rose for the old 15th Company.

Steve Smith.

It was very soon afterwards that Portsmouth itself grew out of the soldiers' team, which eventually became a back number and finally extinct. In those days Pompey aimed high. They collected a very classy lot—mostly Scotsmen—and challenged for the Southern League at once. It was not long before the salmon shirted brigade were recognised as one of the best combinations in the country. A rare number of good men they have had since they challenged Fortune to a fall, notably, and possibly greatest of all, Steve Smith, the erstwhile Aston Villa outside left. Steve was a broth of a boy at a sprint down the line and he could middle to an inch. Short of stature he was nevertheless very speedy, and once away very few backs could overtake him. He made his reputation, of course, with the Villa, and as part of the Wheldon-Smith left wing was partner in a combination the fame of which extended from the Hebrides to the Lizard, and which was selected more than once to represent its country, both in *real* International and Inter-League games. His brother, Will, played as inside to him at Pompey and brought to bear all the old wolf style of play, with its refreshing vigour and directness; but he was not so good as Steve, by a long way. Not in football, anyway. There was a trait about the brothers, though, that was greatly to their credit and kept them the sturdiest pair of players in the country. Whether in Brum, Pompey, or New Brompton, they would not be in the town a fortnight before they had made themselves teachers of a Sunday School class somewhere. Real good fellows they were, and of the sort of stuff to give the manager or directors no trouble at all. Pompey since those days has seen trouble. Under the able captaincy of Buick they should have become great, but somehow they went the other way. Nowadays they appear to have picked up a bit, and we at Millwall in the days of success will wish them a very speedy climb to former greatness.

The "Pilgrims."

Plymouth are different birds. Compared with ourselves they are young, very young, whilst our heads are grey with years. They began about a decade ago, developing out of the "Green Waves" and "Argyle," two amateur clubs that ran alone down on the lovely South-west coast for some considerable time. Arsenal was doing mission work just about then out West and as a result of several professional matches that were fixed up for the education of the Plymouth brethren, it was decided to start a professional team. So, too, at Exeter. Alas! Poor old Arsenal! To think that in the days of their undoing their converts should be flourishing like the green bay tree! But so it is, and woe to us for the old days that will come no more! Plymouth have had some good men in their short career, but the remarkable thing in connection with their players has been the partnership of Atterbury and Butler at back.

The match at Millwall on 24 January 1913 was played two days after the hosts met Portsmouth. This page from the double-match programme highlights the particular style of sports writers at this time – very different to that of their modern counterparts.

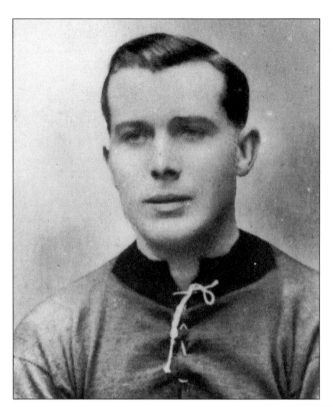

Forward Bert Bowler was playing for the Army Cup winners Sherwood Foresters when discovered by Robert Jack in 1912. After turning professional, Bowler stayed with the club until retiring in 1923.

The team page from Argyle's programme for the 1-1 Southern League draw against Bristol Rovers on 20 September 1913. The Pilgrims fielded a familiar line-up for this match. In this season, Argyle achieved a finishing position of fifth place.

Argyle takes the Biscuit!

IN MEMORY

OF DEAR OLD

READING,

Who fell at
HOME PARK,

in the First Round in the
English Cup,

January 10th, 1920,

to the Evergreen
Plymouth Argyle.

Boldly to the fray they went
On Honour, Fame and Victory bent,
But with sad hearts they came away,
For the Great Match they lost to-day.
Their opponents were far too good,
In fact they stood like logs of wood.
Their day is gone, their time is o'er,
Cup-Tie Matches, this year, they will play no
more.

Here lies a team who did no good,
And if they lived they never would;
Where they have gone, and how
they fare
Nobody knows, and nobody cares.

R.I.P.

The 1919/20 FA Cup campaign saw victories against Reading (2-0) and Barnsley (4-1). With tongue firmly in cheek, a local wag decided to rub salt into the opponents' wounds. However, Round Three turned out to be a different affair with a 3-1 defeat at Huddersfield Town.

IN LOVING MEMORY

OF DEAR OLD

BARNSLEY,

The famous Yorkshire Terriers, who fought to
the death the celebrated Brums, Jan. 10th, 1920.
Owned and trained by Sir W. B. Albion, who in
the next encounter for the English Cup
at Home Park,

January 31st, 1920,

**fell to the famous Bulldog of the
West, Argyle.**

Owned and trained by "The Pilgrims," who
says he is particularly fond of Yorkshire
Puddings and Biscuits. P.S.—Note the Sauce.

Poor old Barnsley, honored be his name,
Poor old Barnsley fought and died true game.
Countless battles he has fought,
Many drawn and won.
His Cup-Tie days are over,
His fighting days are done.
All who read this epitaph
Kindly shed a tear
For the beloved departed
In memory ever dear.—**R.I.P.**

Tune : The Deaf March.
Wailers—Reading and Millwall.

Written and composed by the Lucky Black Cat,
"Old Whiskers," author of "Let 'em all Come"
and "So Say All of Us."
Music by Tom and "Pussyfoot."
Sung by Howler, Growler, Barks, & Snaps.
All bites reserved, and free fights arranged for
at the Cosmo. Gloves can be obtained with
an Argyle Hockey Club.
Ambulance and Undertakers kept waiting.
No delay! Hurry up!

The team, pictured at Millbay Station, ready for the trip to Huddersfield. The train took the party to Leeds for an overnight stop. From left to right, standing (surrounded by well-wishers): J. McCormick, Fred Craig, Billy Kellock, Moses Russell, Bert Bowler, Robert Jack (Secretary Manager), Jimmy Logan, Septimus Atterbury (with arms folded), Tommy Haynes (Trainer), Hubert Papps (Director). Seated: Harry Raymond, Tommy Gallogley, Billy Forbes, Jimmy Dickinson.

Jack 'Ginger' Hill joined the side in 1920 and was a commanding figure at centre half. He made 102 appearances in the first three seasons of League football, before joining Burnley for the huge sum of £6,000. Ginger then progressed to England international honours, including the captaincy of the side.

Three
Into the Football League

THIS IS TO
INTRODUCE
BOB JACK AND
HIS MERRY
MARIONETTES
—THE BIG NOISES
FROM
PLYMOUTH SOUND

Argyle's manager depicted in cartoon form – pulling the strings.

In 1920, Plymouth Argyle became a founder member of the Third Division (South) when all members of the Southern League turned over *en bloc*, with the exception of Cardiff City who had been elected to Division Two. Grimsby Town moved down to the new division. The Southern League then became a competition for the reserve teams. Here is the 1919/20 team photograph – the final season before League football arrived in Plymouth. From left to right, back row: Septimus Atterbury, W. 'Tich' Horne, Fred Craig, Moses Russell. Middle row: J. Harker (Assistant Trainer), Jimmy Dickinson, S. Davis, J. McCormick, H. Wilcox, Billy Forbes, George Frost, Tommy Haynes (Trainer). Front row: W. Bull, Jimmy Kirkpatrick, Tommy Gallogley, Billy Kellock, Arthur Dixon, S. Blott, Jimmy Logan. After finishing eleventh in Division Three (South) in the inaugural League season, the following six were agonising for supporters as the team finished as runners-up in each campaign.

Centre forward Frank Richardson joined The Pilgrims in 1921 from Barking – as did Jack Leslie and Alf Rowe. His forty-one goals in sixty-seven games got off to a flying start with all the goals on the opening day of the 1921/22 season in the 3-1 away win at Bristol Rovers.

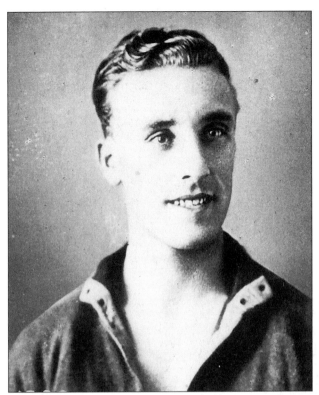

H.G. Batten was affectionately known as 'Bert' during his five seasons at Home Park, having arrived from Bristol City. His seven first team outings in Argyle's second season of League football brought no rewards in front of goal, but that eventually changed and he went on to score twenty-six goals in eighty-six League matches for The Pilgrims. His only hat-trick came on 20 September 1924, in the 4-0 home victory over Luton Town. Selection for the 1925 FA tour of Australia led to interest from First Division Everton, who signed the forward a year later. Alas, he only made occasional appearances for the Toffeemen and, after a single season at Goodison Park, joined Bradford City.

Percy Cherrett signed for The Pilgrims in September 1923, from south coast rivals Portsmouth. He marked his debut by scoring against his former club. The twenty-seven goals he scored before the end of the season were followed by another nine strikes in twenty-one outings during the 1924/25 campaign. Hard to imagine then, that he was a mere reserve team player when Jack Cock came to Argyle. Transferred to Crystal Palace in 1925, Cherrett scored twenty-six times in the thirty-five games of his first full season with the Eagles and totalled an amazing fifty-eight goals in seventy-five League matches for the London side

During the summer of 1924, Plymouth Argyle undertook a venture that was almost unheard of at the time – an overseas tour. Exhibition games were played in Uruguay and the Argentine, causing much interest in Latin-America. Pictured *en route* on board the *R.M.S.P. Avon*, from left to right, back row: Jack Fowler, Bruce Wallace, Leslie Deacon, Patsy Cocoran, Billy Forbes, Percy Cherrett, F.W. Reeve (Football League referee). Middle row: Fred Craig, Jimmy Logan, Cyril Eastwood, Johnny Walker, Bob Preston, Charlie Millar, Jack Leslie, Moses Russell, Bert Batten. Front row: W.W. Wakeling (Director), Frank Sloan, Albert Fishwick, Robert Jack (Manager).

The South American experience brought three wins and three draws from nine games against strong opposition. Here, the travelling party are relaxing over some liquid refreshment at the Buenos Aires power station, two days after the first game of the tour against Portenos. Left to right, back row: Billy Forbes, Fred Cosgrove, Albert Fishwick, Frank Sloan, Mr Brady, Robert Jack, Johnny Walker, Alf Rowe, Bruce Wallace, Leslie Deacon, Jimmy Logan. Middle row: Moses Russell, Bert Batten, Mr Mortimer, Bob Preston. Front row: F.W. Reeve, Charlie Miller, John Smith, W.W. Wakeling, Mr Dunn, Percy Cherrett, Patsy Cocoran, Jack Leslie.

In 1924, a left-winger signed from Scottish junior side Kirkintilloch Rob Roy and made a record 470 League and 22 FA Cup appearances over thirteen years for Argyle. The name of Sammy Black has since been regarded as one of the best, if not *the* best player to pull on a green shirt. After a short spell with Queens Park Rangers, he returned to Plymouth to become a storehouse assistant at the Royal Naval Armament depot. His outstanding contribution there led to his being awarded the Imperial Service Medal in December 1966.

Another signing in that year was John Gilbert Cock, more commonly known as simply 'Jack'. Despite a wound received during the First World War, after which he was awarded the Military Cross for his efforts, Cock scored at an incredible rate. Seventy-two League goals in ninety appearances made the Cornishman, who was signed from Everton, a firm favourite.

No. 1   FEB. 1925

PLYMOUTH ARGYLE
A.F.C.

SUPPORTERS' CLUB

OFFICERS :

Chairman : Mr. A. E. CLOAD

Vice-Chairman : Mr. S. MARTIN

Hon. Secretary: Mr. E. WALLACE,
30 Staddon Terrace, Plymouth.

Asst. Secretary : Mr. W. BELL

Hon. Treasurer : Mr. W. JUTSON

Published by the Plymouth Argyle Supporters' Club.

LOOK OUT FOR SOCIAL PROGRAMME

On Thursday 22 January 1925, a meeting was convened at the Kirton Hall, Park Street, where it was decided to form the Plymouth Argyle Supporters' Club. Initially viewed with suspicion, regarding the benefits that such a body could bring to Plymouth Argyle, early prejudices were overcome through sincere endeavour. From small beginnings it progressed to be recognised as an organisation that was adhering to its motto – 'To Help Not Hinder' – and maintained the goodwill of the supporters in harmony with the interests of the football club. A month after the Supporters' Club was formed, the first publicity leaflet was printed, containing many useful tips.

The first Argyle side to win promotion within the Football League finished the 1929/30 Division Three (South) campaign as Champions, with an unbeaten home record. From left to right, back row: Moses Russell, Harry Bland, Norman Mackay, Fred Craig, Fred McKenzie, Freddie Titmuss, Alec Hardie, Tommy Haynes (Trainer). Front row: Alf Matthews, Tommy Grozier, Frank Sloan, Jack Vidler, Ray Bowden, Jack Leslie, Sammy Black. Inset: Harry Cann (left) and John Pullen. Argyle, since the 1921/22 season, had become the 'nearly team'. After finishing second in Division Three (South) for six consecutive campaigns, they went on to finish third and fourth before finally achieving the reward of Division Two football.

Four
The Thriving Thirties

W. Taylor, the sports editor of the *Western Independent*, published this souvenir booklet. The 1929/30 season and those involved with it were featured in the finest possible detail to provide supporters with an informative keepsake of a memorable side.

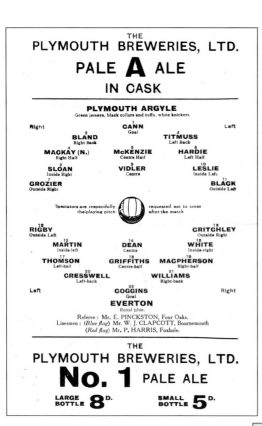

THE

PLYMOUTH BREWERIES, LTD.

PALE **A** ALE

IN CASK

PLYMOUTH ARGYLE
Green jerseys, black collars and cuffs, white knickers

Right		CANN		Left
		Goal		
	BLAND		TITMUSS	
	Right Back		Left Back	
MACKAY (N.)		McKENZIE		HARDIE
Right Half		Centre Half		Left Half
SLOAN		VIDLER		LESLIE
Inside Right		Centre		Inside Left
GROZIER				BLACK
Outside Right				Outside Left

Spectators are respectfully requested not to cross the playing pitch after the match

RIGBY				CRITCHLEY
Outside Left				Outside Right
MARTIN		DEAN		WHITE
Inside-left		Centre		Inside-right
THOMSON		GRIFFITHS		MACPHERSON
Left-half		Centre-half		Right-half
CRESSWELL				WILLIAMS
Left-back				Right-back
Left		COGGINS		Right
		Goal		

EVERTON
Royal Blue.

Referee : Mr. E. PINCKSTON, Four Oaks.
Linesmen : (*Blue flag*) Mr. W. J. CLAPCOTT, Bournemouth
(*Red flag*) Mr. P. HARRIS, Foxhole.

THE

PLYMOUTH BREWERIES, LTD.

No. **1** PALE ALE

| LARGE BOTTLE **8**D. | | SMALL BOTTLE **5**D. |

On 30 August 1930, newly relegated Everton visited Home Park to face the newly promoted Pilgrims. The Merseyside club boasted five internationals, including the legendary William Ralph (Dixie) Dean. The game attracted a crowd of 34,916 and there were some 1,200 cars from all over Devon and Cornwall in the fine new car park, which was in use for the first time. Argyle lost 3-2, but played extremely well against such strong opposition. From the centre spread of the match programme, note that the Argyle players are numbered one to eleven and the Everton players twelve to twenty-two.

Scoring ten goals for Looe in a match against Tavistock was enough to persuade Robert Jack that Ray Bowden was a striker he could ill-afford to ignore. Three years later he had collected a Division Three (South) Championship medal, having contributed eighteen goals. Selection for the FA touring party to Canada in 1931 saw the Cornishman score five goals in the first game and it was clear that he would go on to bigger things. Bowden's eighty-three goals in 143 League matches led Herbert Chapman to pay an Arsenal record fee of £4,500 to take him to Highbury and an immediate League Championship was secured. The title was retained in the 1933/34 season, with Bowden the joint top scorer with Cliff Bastin. After the Championship hat-trick, success in the FA Cup Final of 1936 saw his last honour before a £5,000 move to Newcastle United. On retiring from football, he returned to Plymouth with six England caps to his name and opened a sports shop in the city.

A former Cornwall County player, goalkeeper Harry Cann arrived at Home Park in 1928, having played Duchy League soccer with Tintagel. He gained a regular place in the side in March 1929 and held it until the arrival of Bill Harper in November 1931. He regained the number one shirt two years later. Cann was in goal on the occasion of the club's heaviest defeat at that point in their history, 9-1 against Everton on 27 December 1930 – four of the goals were scored by 'Dixie' Dean. However, observers readily agreed that without his bravery and agility, the scoreline would have been even more embarrassing, hence the standing ovation he received after the match. After 225 League appearances, he joined Fulham in 1939.

In 1931, half back Archie Gorman joined Plymouth Argyle from Edinburgh City and began a long professional career at Home Park that went beyond his playing days. The Second World War brought a halt to 240 League matches, although he was able to compete in the South West Regional League in the 1939/40 season. The 1945/46 campaign enabled Gorman to play in sixteen Southern League games. At the resumption of Football League action he was appointed as the assistant to trainer Bill Harper and completed a trainer's course, sponsored by the FA.

Born in London and the son of a Jamaican, Jack Leslie left Barking to become Argyle's first coloured player in 1921. His on-field exploits with Sammy Black became legendary, and many felt he would have been an asset to the national side. Indeed, manager Robert Jack received 'official word' that Leslie was to play for England, but formal notification was never received. Many felt that his exclusion was purely due to the colour of his skin. Leslie retired in 1934, having scored 131 goals in 383 League matches.

Right-winger Alf Matthews joined Bristol City as an amateur in 1921 and enjoyed early success in the Southern League as well as winning a Gloucestershire County cap. A year after turning professional, he joined Exeter City, for whom he made 145 League appearances (including a club record 117 consecutive matches) and scored 33 goals. However, the time he spent there was not all plain sailing: a fire in the St James Park stand accounted for Matthew's kit and boots, leading to the painful experience of having to break in new footwear. In March 1926, he signed for Argyle, with only injury interrupting another fine unbroken run of ninety games. After promotion to Division Two, he played for another three seasons before retiring with a benefit game against The Grecians. The Bristolian was an all-round sportsman who spent his summer playing bowls and, if the weather prevented that, he could be found swinging his golf clubs at Yelverton.

From 1930, right-back Harry Roberts played in 248 League matches in which he scored twenty-one goals, mostly from penalties. A gritty Yorkshireman, Roberts came to Plymouth from his first club, Leeds United. His take-no-prisoners approach often led to him attracting the attention of referees and his hard-man image was consolidated with bouts of all-in wrestling. His association with Argyle ended with a transfer to Bristol Rovers in 1937.

Having gained experience with Hibernian and Aston Villa, Norman Mackay played for Lovell's Athletic and earned his living selling the famous Lovell's toffees until signing for Argyle in 1927. Following a brief run in the reserves, his first League match – the Division Three (South) home meeting with Coventry City – saw him bag a second half hat-trick in atrocious weather. Over the next seven years, the Scotsman played in 227 League matches for The Pilgrims, scoring fourteen goals.

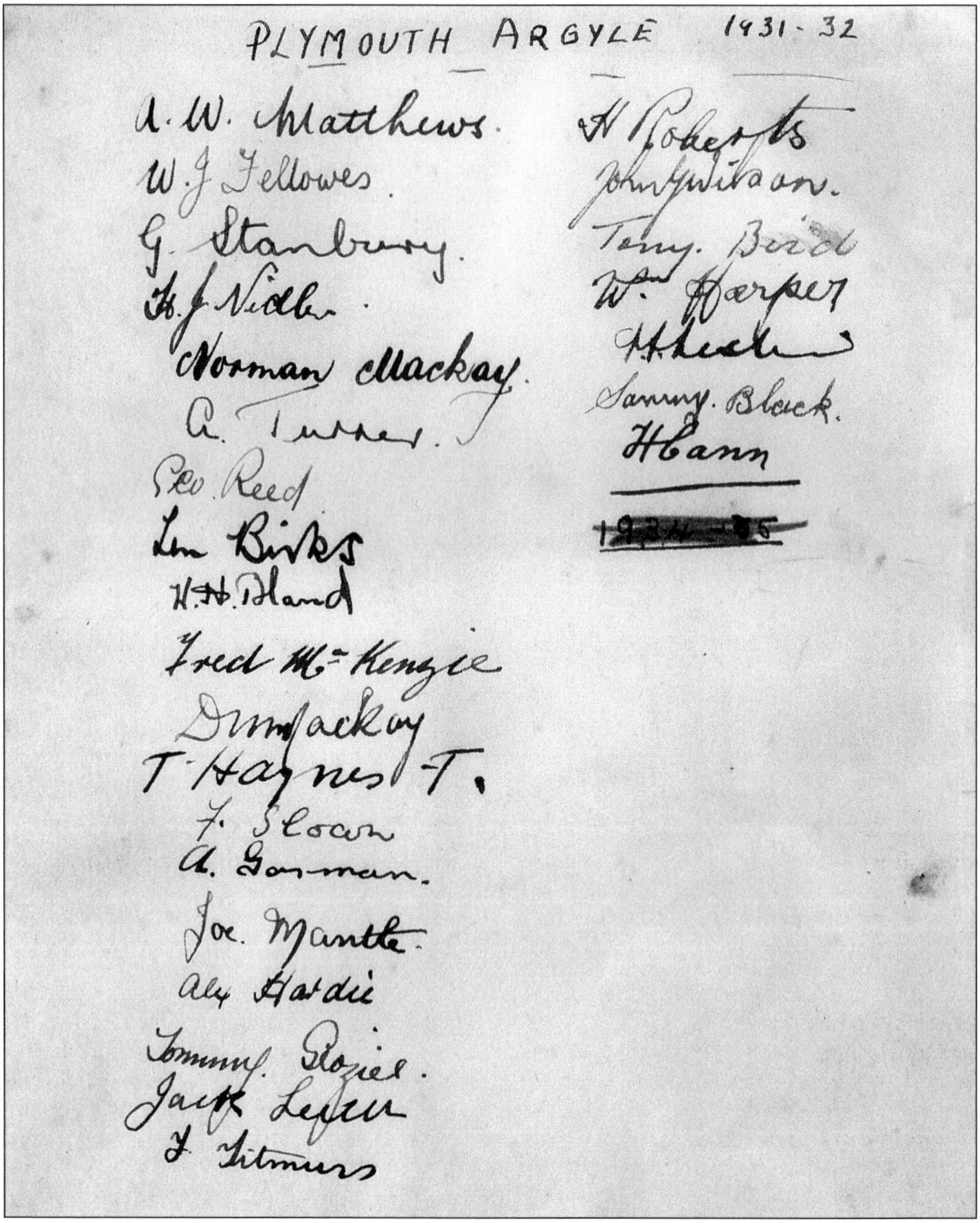

PLYMOUTH ARGYLE   1931-32

A. W. Matthews.
W. J. Fellowes.
G. Stanbury.
F. J. Nicol.
Norman Mackay.
A. Turner.
Geo. Reed
Len Birks
H. H. Bland
Fred McKenzie
Dunfackey
T. Haynes T.
F. Slocon
A. Gorman.
Joe. Mantle.
Aly Hardie
Tommy. Rogers.
Jack Leslie
F. Titmuss

H. Roberts
John Guilson.
Tony. Bird
Wm. Harper
H. Heale
Sammy. Black.
H. Cann

1931-32

The signatures of one of the most famous teams to wear the green of Plymouth Argyle.

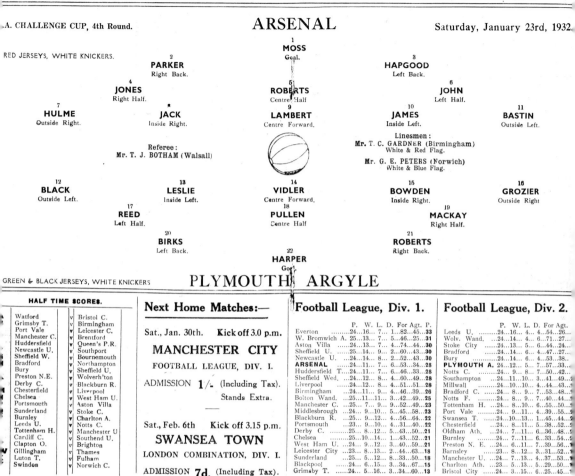

.A. CHALLENGE CUP, 4th Round. **ARSENAL** Saturday, January 23rd, 1932.

RED JERSEYS, WHITE KNICKERS.

1
MOSS
Goal.

2
PARKER
Right Back.

3
HAPGOOD
Left Back.

4
JONES
Right Half.

5
ROBERTS
Centre Half

6
JOHN
Left Half.

7
HULME
Outside Right.

8
JACK
Inside Right.

9
LAMBERT
Centre Forward.

10
JAMES
Inside Left.

11
BASTIN
Outside Left.

Linesmen :
Mr. T. C. GARDNER (Birmingham)
White & Red Flag.

Mr. G. E. PETERS (Norwich)
White & Blue Flag.

Referee :
Mr. T. J. BOTHAM (Walsall)

12
BLACK
Outside Left.

13
LESLIE
Inside Left.

14
VIDLER
Centre Forward.

15
BOWDEN
Inside Right.

16
GROZIER
Outside Right

17
REED
Left Half.

18
PULLEN
Centre Half

19
MACKAY
Right Half.

20
BIRKS
Left Back.

21
ROBERTS
Right Back.

22
HARPER
Goal.

PLYMOUTH ARGYLE

GREEN & BLACK JERSEYS, WHITE KNICKERS

HALF TIME SCORES.

	v	
Watford	v	Bristol C.
Grimsby T.	v	Birmingham
Port Vale	v	Brentford
Manchester C.	v	Queen's P.R.
Huddersfield	v	Southport
Newcastle U.	v	Bournemouth
Sheffield W.	v	Northampton
Bradford	v	Sheffield U.
Bury	v	Wolverh'ton
Preston N.E.	v	Blackburn R.
Derby C.	v	Liverpool
Chesterfield	v	West Ham U.
Chelsea	v	Aston Villa
Portsmouth	v	Stoke C.
Sunderland	v	Charlton A.
Burnley	v	Notts C.
Leeds U.	v	Manchester U
Tottenham H.	v	Southend U.
Cardiff C.	v	Brighton
Clapton O.	v	Thames
Gillingham	v	Fulham
Luton T.	v	Norwich C.
Swindon	v	

Next Home Matches:—

Sat., Jan. 30th.   Kick off 3.0 p.m.

MANCHESTER CITY

FOOTBALL LEAGUE, DIV. I.

ADMISSION **1/-** (Including Tax).
Stands Extra.

Sat., Feb. 6th   Kick off 3.15 p.m.

SWANSEA TOWN

LONDON COMBINATION, DIV. I.

ADMISSION **7d.** (Including Tax).

Football League, Div. 1.

	P.	W.	L.	D.	For	Agt.	P.
Everton	24	16	7	1	82	45	33
W. Bromwich A.	25	13	7	5	46	25	31
Aston Villa	24	13	7	4	74	44	30
Sheffield U.	25	14	9	2	60	43	30
Newcastle U.	24	14	8	2	52	43	30
ARSENAL	24	11	7	6	53	34	28
Huddersfield T.	24	11	7	6	46	33	28
Sheffield Wed.	24	12	8	4	60	49	28
Liverpool	24	12	8	4	51	51	28
Birmingham	24	11	9	4	46	39	26
Bolton Wand.	25	11	11	3	42	49	25
Manchester C.	25	7	9	9	52	49	23
Middlesbrough	24	9	10	5	45	58	23
Blackburn R.	25	9	12	4	56	64	22
Portsmouth	23	9	10	4	31	40	22
Derby C.	25	8	12	5	43	50	21
Chelsea	25	10	14	1	43	52	21
West Ham U.	24	9	12	3	45	59	21
Leicester City	23	8	13	2	44	63	18
Sunderland	25	5	12	8	33	50	18
Blackpool	24	6	15	3	34	67	15
Grimsby T.	24	5	16	3	34	60	13

Football League, Div. 2.

	P.	W.	L.	D.	For	Agt.
Leeds U.	24	16	4	4	54	26
Wolv. Wand.	24	14	4	6	71	27
Stoke City	24	13	5	6	44	24
Bradford	24	14	6	4	47	27
Bury	24	6	4	53	38	
PLYMOUTH A.	24	12	5	7	57	33
Notts C.	24	9	8	7	50	42
Southampton	24	11	10	3	41	49
Millwall	24	10	10	4	44	43
Bradford C.	24	8	9	7	53	48
Notts F.	24	8	9	7	40	44
Tottenham H.	24	8	10	6	55	50
Port Vale	24	9	11	4	39	55
Swansea T.	24	10	13	1	45	44
Chesterfield	24	8	11	5	38	52
Oldham Ath.	24	7	11	6	36	48
Burnley	24	7	11	6	33	54
Preston N. E.	24	6	11	7	39	56
Barnsley	23	8	12	3	31	52
Manchester U.	24	7	13	4	57	52
Charlton Ath.	23	5	13	5	29	50
Bristol City	24	3	15	6	25	45

The FA Cup campaign of 1931/32 drew Arsenal, the current Champions who finished the season as runners-up in Division One, against the Argyle side who had beaten Manchester United in Round One. The Gunners won the Second Round tie 4-2 in front of 65,386 spectators – a Highbury record – leaving thousands locked outside half an hour before kick-off. Many familiar names graced the Arsenal side, but it was a special day for Plymouth 'keeper Bill Harper, making a return visit to the club with whom he had won a Championship medal in the previous season under Herbert Chapman. The match referee was to be Mr Wiltshire from Exeter, but Arsenal requested that a new official be appointed, as he lived in the same county as their opponents.

Ready to start on the bread rolls at a dinner given by the Supporters' Club in September 1932. After posing for this photo, the team manager and directors duly took their seats at the top table: A.H. Cole, Robert Jack, Hubert Papps, Lieut-Col. R.V. Hunt, E. Elliot Square, A.C. Ballard, T. R. Nicholls, Alfred Gard, Edgar F. Wallace, W.H. Sloman, Alf Matthews, William Olden, J. Dustan.

The menu card from the historic first *annual* dinner of the Supporters' Club, held six months later.

Plymouth Argyle Supporters Club

⊏⊐

FIRST

ANNUAL DINNER

CO-OPERATIVE CAFÉ
COURTENAY STREET
. . PLYMOUTH . .

⊏⊐

March 21st, 1933   7.30 p.m.

. Menu .

SOUP
Tomato or Ox Tail, with Rolls

FISH
Boiled or Fried

JOINTS
Roast Beef, Yorkshire Pudding
Roast Mutton, Red Jelly
Roast Pork, Onion or Apple Sauce

VEGETABLES
Boiled or Baked Potatoes
Cauliflower, White Sauce
Peas and Turnips

SWEETS
Fruit Tarts and Cream
Fruit Salad and Cream
Fruit Jellies and Trifles
Cheese and Biscuits
Coffee

. Toast List .

"The King"
Proposed by .. .. The Chairman

"Plymouth Argyle Supporters Club"
Proposed by .. .. .. E. Elliot Square, Esq.
Response by .. .. .. T. R. Nicholls, Esq.

"Plymouth Argyle Football Co. Ltd. and Team"
Proposed by .. .. .. Edgar F. Wallace, Esq.
Response by .. .. .. Robert Jack, Esq.

"Kindred Organisations"
Proposed by .. .. .. W. H. Sloman, Esq.
Response by .. C. S. Hill, Esq., *Hon. Sec.* D.C.F.A.
And Representatives of Plymouth Speed-
ways and Albion Supporters Club.

"City of Plymouth"
Proposed by .. .. .. W. C. Johnson, Esq.
Response by .. .. .. The Mayor of Plymouth
(Alderman R. R. Oke)

The menu shows the veritable feast on offer – worthy of the occasion.

Official Programme 2d.

Home Park, Plymouth   Saturday, Jan. 28th, 1933

PLYMOUTH ARGYLE

VERSUS

FIRST VIENNA CLUB

Kick-off **3·0** p.m.

THE MATCH OF THE SEASON!

It was billed as the match of the season: Austrian League Champions and Central European Cup winners First Club Vienna came to Plymouth for a friendly match on 28 January 1933. They brought a squad that contained no less than twelve internationals.

PLYMOUTH ARGYLE

Colours—Green jerseys black collars and cuffs, white knickers

Right   Left

1
HARPER
Goal

2   3
ROBERTS   RAE
Right-back   Left-back

4   5   6
MACKAY   McKENZIE   GORMAN
Right-half   Centre-half   Left-half
8   9   10
BOWDEN   MELANIPHY   LESLIE
Inside-right   Centre   Inside-left
7   11
GROZIER   BLACK
Outside-right   Outside-left

Spectators are respectfully requested not to cross the playing pitch after the match

12   16
F. SCHONWETTER   A. BROSENBAUER
Outside-left   Outside-right

13   14   15
S. WORTMAN   F. GSCHWEIDL   J. ADELBRECHT
Inside-left   Centre   Inside-right
17   18   19
L. MACHU   L. HOFMANN   O. KALLER
Left-half   Centre-half   Right-half
20   21
J. BLUM or W. SCHMAUS   K. RAINER or J. BLUM
Left-back   Right-back

Left   22   Right
           K. HORESCHOFSKY
                  Goal

THE FIRST VIENNA PLAYERS

Colours—Yellow Jerseys, Blue Knickers.

Referee—Mr. H. F. FORD, Exeter.

Linesmen—(*red flag*) Chief Writer J. MOLYNEUX, R.N.
(*blue flag*) Mr. W. H. GAYTON, Plympton.

The official team photograph taken at the start of the 1933/34 season which began with a 4-0 home win over Manchester United and also contained a draw with the mighty Huddersfield Town in the FA Cup, watched by a record attendance of 43,426. From left to right, back row: Tommy Black, Harry Bland, Harry Cann, Harry Roberts, Bill Harper, Jimmy Rae, John Milne, L. Woosey. Middle row: Septimus Atterbury (Assistant Trainer), Peter Simpson, Jack Pullen, Norman Mackay, Bob Carter, George Forrest, George Reed, Fred McKenzie, Will Godfrey, Alec Hardie, Tommy Haynes (Trainer). Front row: Tony Bird, Jack Demellweek, Tommy Grozier, Frank Sloan, George Briggs, Jimmy Cookson, Robert Jack (Manager), Eugene Melaniphy, Jack Leslie, Reg Bungay, Jack Vidler. Seated on grass: Sammy Black, Archie Gorman.

A FEW THUMB-NAIL SKETCHES ON TO-DAY'S VISITORS

TURNER, Hugh (*Goalkeeper*). A native of Wigan. Previously played with High Fell. Turner has given some brilliant displays in goal for the Yorkshire Club, and has represented England against France and Belgium. Height 5 ft. 10 ins. Weight 12 st. 8 lbs.

GOODALL, Roy (*right-back*). Born Dronfield Woodhouse, and played for the senior club of that district. Goodall is very accurate with long clearances, and strong under pressure. Tackles fearlessly and very quick in recovery. Goodall played for England against Scotland in 1926–27–28–30–31 ; against Wales in 1928–31 ; against Ireland in 1931–32–33 ; against France and Belgium in 1927–28 ; against Germany and Austria 1930 ; against Belgium in 1931 ; and against Austria, Italy and Sweden in 1933. Height 5 ft. 11 ins. Weight 12 st. 7 lbs.

ROUGHTON, William (*left-back*). A native of Manchester. Formerly an engineer. Very clever in anticipation, and strong in defence. Height 6 ft. Weight 11 st. 7 lbs.

CARR, William (*right half-back*). Born Horden, and previously played with the club of that district. Regarded as being very clever in attack, and reliable in defence. Height 5 ft. 8½ ins. Weight 11 st. Carr has recently taken the place of Willingham, who has been on the injured list.

WILLINGHAM, Kenneth. A native of Sheffield, who was unfortunate to be injured when on the verge of International honours. Willingham previously played with Worksop Town, and is a Sheffield Schoolboys' Sprint champion. Height 5 ft. 8 ins. Weight 11 st. 8 lbs.

CHRISTIE, Norman (*centre-half-back*). Born at Jarrow. Has played for Bishop Auckland. Plays a consistently good game in any position in the intermediate line. Has a penchant for opening up the game with long sweeping passes. Height 5 ft. 10 ins. Weight 11 st. 7 lbs. Has a rival for the position in

YOUNG, Alfred. A native of Sunderland, who previously played with Durham City. Young is very strong in defence, and is an English Internationalist, having played against Wales last Season. Height 6 ft. Weight 12 st.

CAMPBELL, Austin, F. (*left half-back*). A native of Leadgate. Campbell is renowned for the great game he played for Blackburn Rovers in the Cup Final of 1927–28 when they defeated Huddersfield Town 3–1. Campbell played for England against Ireland and Wales in 1929 ; against Scotland, Ireland and Wales in 1931, and against Ireland and Wales in 1932. Height 5 ft. 9 ins. Weight 11 st. 10 lb.

WILLIAMS (*outside-right*). Born Aberdare. Previously played for Llanelly. Height 5 ft. 6 ins. Weight 10 st. 7 lbs.

SMITH, William, H. (*outside-right or left*). Born Tantobie, Co. Durham. Made his name as an outside-left, and was one of the fastest wingers in the game. Although regarded as the veteran in the team, Smith continues to play extraordinarily well, and retains his long stride. Is an English Internationalist. Height 5 ft. 10 ins. Weight 11 st. 2 lbs.

McLEAN, George (*inside-right*). A native of Forfar. Previously played with Forfar Athletic and Bradford. A schemer of the first order. Possesses a strong shot, but is better occupied in creating openings for others. Height 5 ft. 7 ins. Weight 11 st.

MANGNALL, David (*centre-forward*). A native of Maltby, and had trials with Doncaster Rovers and Rotherham United, his last Club being Leeds United. Mangnall is fast, and has a deceptive body swerve. Height 5 ft. 10 ins. Weight 11 st. 9 lbs. Mangnall has been on the injured list recently, and his place has been filled by J. Smith

SMITH, John. A native of Dewsbury. Smith is very fast and clever, and is regarded in Yorkshire as the most promising young player found for the position for many years. Height 5 ft. 11 ins. Weight 11 st. 6 lbs.

LUKE, Charles (*inside or outside-left*). Is another player in which Bishop Auckland prides itself. Luke is a natural player with speed and endless resource. Is tricky and plucky. Height 5 ft. 7 ins. Weight 11 st. He is proving an ideal partner for

BOTT, Wilfred (*outside-left or right*). Bott is a native of Doncaster, and has played for Doncaster Rovers. Possesses skill combined with speed and usually very accurate with his centres and shooting. Height 5 ft. 7 ins. Weight 11 st. 2 lbs.

The team page and pen pictures (then known as thumbnail sketches) of the Huddersfield team. Following a 1-1 draw at Home Park, the side on their way to a runners-up place in Division One recorded a decisive 6-2 victory over Argyle.

Reserve team programmes were replaced with single page team sheets a long time ago. Before the Second World War, full programmes were issued to supporters who watched the second string, illustrated by this fine example from September 1933.

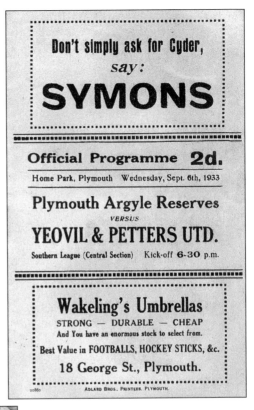

Reg Bungay only made two first team appearances, but each player was afforded the luxury of a complimentary season ticket, normally used by a relative of the player to whom it was issued. Note that holes were punched from the relevant match numbers upon entry to the stadium.

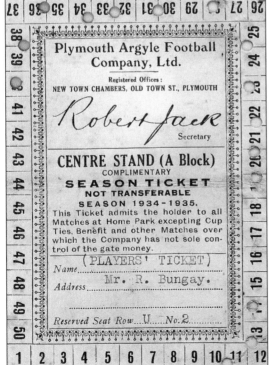

49

Some of the Argyle stars of the early 1930s – this time depicted in ink.

Robert Jack's side of 1934/35 brought moderate success with a finishing position of eighth in Division Two. This team photo was taken during the early part of the campaign. From left to right, back row: Archie Gorman, Jack Demellweek, Harry Roberts, Harry Cann, Johnny McNeill, Tommy Black, Jimmy Rae. Front row: Tommy Grozier, Frank Sloan, George Briggs, Sammy Black, Jack Vidler.

The issue of shares in 1935 invited supporters to apply for an allocation – as long as each form was completed distinctly in block capital letters and each woman stated whether she was a spinster, wife or widow. At five shillings apiece, 50,271 shares were issued.

THIS FORM SHOULD BE FILLED UP AND FORWARDED together with a remittance for the amount payable on application to NATIONAL PROVINCIAL BANK, LIMITED, Bedford Street, Plymouth, or any of its Branches in Devon and Cornwal

No.

PLYMOUTH ARGYLE FOOTBALL COMPA
LIMITED

Issue of 50,271 Ordinary Shares of 5/- each

FORM OF APPLICATION

To the Directors of the
PLYMOUTH ARGYLE FOOTBALL COMPANY, LIMITED.

Gentlemen,

I/we enclose cheque for the sum of £ .... being payment on application for .... shares and I/we apply for and request you to allot to me/us that number of shares upon the terms of the Company's Prospectus dated 11th July, 1935, and I/we hereby undertake and agree to accept such shares, or any less number that may be allotted to me/us. And I/we authorise you to place my/our name(s) on the register of the Company as the holder(s) of the said shares.

Please write distinctly. State Title (if any) or whether Mr., Mrs. or Miss.

Usual Signature ....

PLEASE WRITE DISTINCTLY AND IN BLOCK CAPITAL LETTERS	Surname ....
	Christian Name or Names .... (IN FULL)
	Permanent Address .... for registration purposes (IN FULL) ....
	Occupation or Description ....

Date .... 1935.

(A woman should simply state whether she is a spinster, wife or widow).

N.B.—In case of joint application, all applicants must sign.

Cheques should be made payable to "BEARER" and crossed "NOT NEGOTIABLE." If altered from "ORDER" to "BEARER" the alteration must be SIGNED by the drawer of the cheque. No receipt for the amount paid will be issued, but in due course letter of acceptance will be sent.

ADLAND BROS., PRINTERS PLYMOUTH 27419

The visit to Chelsea on 25 January 1936 occurred five days after the death of King George V. The match programme paid tribute to the passing of the King and included a picture of his visit to the London club in 1920.

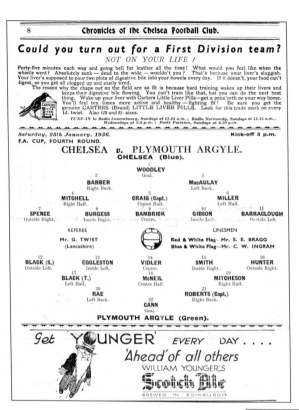

Saturday, 25th January, 1936.   Kick-off 3 p.m.
F.A. CUP, FOURTH ROUND.

CHELSEA v. PLYMOUTH ARGYLE.
CHELSEA (Blue).

1 WOODLEY Goal.

2 BARBER Right Back.   3 MacAULAY Left Back.

4 MITCHELL Right Half.   5 CRAIG (Capt.) Centre Half.   6 MILLER Left Half.

7 SPENCE Outside Right.   8 BURGESS Inside Right.   9 BAMBRICK Centre.   10 GIBSON Inside Left.   11 BARRACLOUGH Outside Left.

REFEREE   LINESMEN
Mr. G. TWIST (Lancashire)   Red & White Flag—Mr. S. E. BRAGG
Blue & White Flag—Mr. C. W. INGRAM

12 BLACK (S.) Outside Left.   13 EGGLESTON Inside Left.   15 VIDLER Centre.   15 SMITH Inside Right.   16 HUNTER Outside Right.

17 BLACK (T.) Left Half.   18 McNEIL Centre Half.   19 MITCHESON Right Half.

20 RAE Left Back.   21 ROBERTS (Capt.) Right Back.

22 CANN Goal.

PLYMOUTH ARGYLE (Green).

A record Home Park League attendance of 43,596 squeezed in to see the unbeaten-at-home Pilgrims draw 2-2 with the recently relegated Aston Villa, a side containing no fewer than six internationals. At least those who arrived in plenty of time for the kick-off were fully entertained, as this programme of pre-match music proves.

Programme of Music : Saturday, Oct. 10, 1936
THE BAND OF
H.M. ROYAL MARINES
PLYMOUTH DIVISION

By kind permission of **Brigadier H. G. GRANT**, commanding Royal Marines, Plymouth, and Officers.
Director of Music : Captain F. J. RICKETTS, R.M.

COMMUNITY SINGING. Compere : **Harry Grose**
Conductor : **Douglas M. Durston** (Plymouth College of Music)

1-30   Selection by Band—" On with the Show " ....arr. Nicholls
1-40   Compère.
1-45   Community Singing
2-0   Selection by Band—" Follow the Fleet " .... Irving Berlin
2-10   Compère.
2-15   Community Singing
2-30   March by Band—" Espana " ....Waldteufel
2-40   Compère.
2-45   Community Singing

1 " The more we are together."
2 " Hearts of Oak "
3 " There's a long, long trail."
4 " Tipperary."
5 " Pack up your troubles."
6 " Love's old sweet song."
7 " One man went to mow."
8 "Shoe fine boy " (new Fox-trot).
9 " There's a tavern in the town."
10 " All through the night."
11 " John Brown's Body."
12 " Land of Hope and Glory."
13 " All the nice girls love a sailor."
14 " Minstrel Boy."
15 " Drink to me only."
16 " Abide with me."

3-0   March by Band—" Colonel Bogey on Parade " ....Alford
GOD SAVE THE KING

During the interval the Band will play a Selection of Popular Airs.

TIME PERMITTING RECORDS WILL BE PLAYED FROM THE FOLLOWING ITEMS FROM " His Master's Voice " CATALOGUE.

Catal. Nos.
B4008   Jollity on the Mountains.
     Viennese Singing Birds.
C1397   In a Monastery Garden.
     Romance.
C2715   Arcadians' Selection. Part 1 and 11.
C2712   Leo Fall Pot Pourri. Part 1 and 11.
C2961   The Rose.
     Selection of English Melodies.

Catal. Nos.
B3951   Parade of Tin Soldiers.
     Wood Nymphs.
C2092   Tales of Hoffman Selection.
C1756   Rose Marie Selection. Part 1 and 11.
K712   Gilbert & Sullivan Medley.
C1335   Light Cavalry.
     Der Freischutz Overture.

The Programme of Records this afternoon has been arranged and provided by Messrs. Moon & Sons (Pianos), Ltd., George Street, Plymouth.

The squad gathered together in the summer before the 1938/39 season. Jack Tresadern is in charge, following the retirement of Robert Jack. Tresadern was a man of great experience, having played for West Ham United in the first Wembley Cup Final in addition to representing England. He arrived in Plymouth after resigning as manager of Tottenham Hotspur. Back row, left to right: Sam Kirkwood, Jimmy Clark, John Murray, O. Roberts, Arthur Davies, Johnny McNeil, Jimmy Rae, Tommy Black, Charlie Fletcher. Middle row: D. Wall (Trainer), Bill Hullett, J. Girvan, Harry Lane, I. Roberts, Harry Cann, Jim McColgan, J. McHarg, Alec Dyer, Tommy Ryan, Bill Harper (Trainer). Front row: Archie Gorman, Bill Olver, Jackie Wharton, Tommy Dougan, Dave Thomas, Jack Tresadern (Secretary Manager), Henry Brown, Jackie Smith, Fred Mitcheson, Jimmy Hunter, Jack Vidler. Seated: F. Duhig, Jim Mailey.

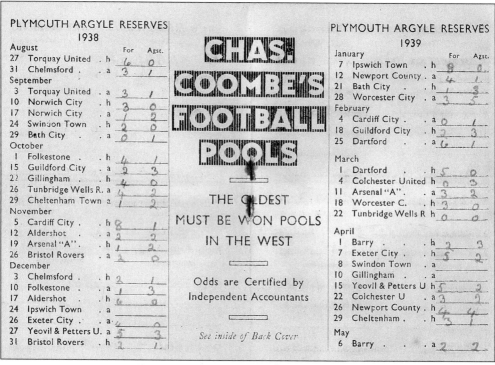

PLYMOUTH ARGYLE RESERVES 1938		For	Agst.
August			
27 Torquay United . h		6	0
31 Chelmsford . . a		3	1
September			
3 Torquay United . a		3	1
10 Norwich City . h		3	0
17 Norwich City . a		1	2
24 Swindon Town . h		2	0
29 Bath City . . a		0	1
October			
1 Folkestone . . h		4	1
15 Guildford City . a		2	3
22 Gillingham . h		4	0
26 Tunbridge Wells R. a		4	2
29 Cheltenham Town a		1	2
November			
5 Cardiff City . . h		8	1
12 Aldershot . . a		2	2
19 Arsenal "A". . h		1	2
26 Bristol Rovers . a		2	0
December			
3 Chelmsford . . h		2	1
10 Folkestone . . a		1	3
17 Aldershot . . h		6	0
24 Ipswich Town . . a			
26 Exeter City . . a		4	0
27 Yeovil & Petters U. a		5	3
31 Bristol Rovers . h		2	1

PLYMOUTH ARGYLE RESERVES 1939		For	Agst.
January			
7 Ipswich Town . h		8	0
12 Newport County . a		4	1
21 Bath City . . h		1	3
28 Worcester City . a		3	5
February			
4 Cardiff City . . a		0	1
18 Guildford City . h		2	3
25 Dartford . . a		6	1
March			
1 Dartford . . h		5	0
4 Colchester United h		0	3
11 Arsenal "A" . . a		3	2
18 Worcester C. . h		3	0
22 Tunbridge Wells R h		0	0
April			
1 Barry . . . h		2	3
7 Exeter City . . h		5	2
8 Swindon Town . a			
10 Gillingham . . a			
15 Yeovil & Petters U h		5	2
22 Colchester U . a		3	2
26 Newport County . h		4	4
29 Cheltenham . . h		3	1
May			
6 Barry . . . a		2	2

CHAS. COOMBE'S FOOTBALL POOLS

THE OLDEST

MUST BE WON POOLS

IN THE WEST

Odds are Certified by

Independent Accountants

See inside of Back Cover

PLYMOUTH ARGYLE
SUPPORTERS' CLUB

MANCHESTER CITY
●
Versus
●
PLYMOUTH ARGYLE

——— AT MANCHESTER ———

Saturday, February 18th

——— 1939 ———

The Committee of the Plymouth Argyle Supporters' Club beg to announce particulars of their Excursion to MANCHESTER by G.W.R. Corridor Express on Friday night, February 17th, 1939.

The approximate times are as follows :

Depart Plymouth (Millbay) 10 p.m.
Arrive Manchester (Mayfield) 6–15 a.m.
Depart Manchester (Mayfield) 12 (midnight)
Arrive Plymouth (Millbay) 8–15 a.m.

Return Fare 19/3

The above times are not applicable to passengers for whom reservations have been made. These passengers will be further advised.

Seats may be booked, or compartments for six or eight persons may be reserved, without extra charge on application to the Secretary. Saloons to accommodate 30 or 40 persons may be obtained at an extra cost of 30/-, but early application is essential.

Supporters were invited to keep meticulous records of matches by purchasing *Dutton's (of Devonport) Football Diary*. Taken from the twelfth season of the publication, for the 1938/39 campaign, these centre pages were set aside for recording results of reserve team football. First team matches were detailed throughout the rest of the pocket-sized book.

The Supporters' Club made every effort to ensure the team were well supported when playing away from home. On this occasion, the reward for those who travelled was a welcome 3-1 win.

Five

The War Years

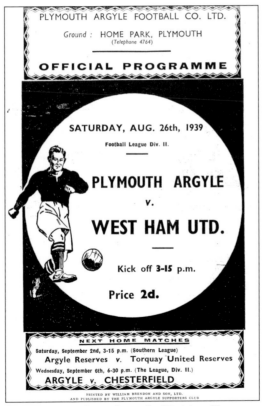

PLYMOUTH ARGYLE FOOTBALL CO. LTD.

Ground : HOME PARK, PLYMOUTH
(Telephone 4764)

OFFICIAL PROGRAMME

SATURDAY, AUG. 26th, 1939

Football League Div. II.

PLYMOUTH ARGYLE

v.

WEST HAM UTD.

Kick off 3-15 p.m.

Price 2d.

NEXT HOME MATCHES
Saturday, September 2nd, 3-15 p.m. (Southern League)
Argyle Reserves v. Torquay United Reserves
Wednesday, September 6th, 6-30 p.m. (The League, Div. II.)
ARGYLE v. CHESTERFIELD

PRINTED BY WILLIAM BRENDON AND SON, LTD.
AND PUBLISHED BY THE PLYMOUTH ARGYLE SUPPORTERS CLUB

The cover of the match programme from the only Division Two match held at Home Park during the 1939/40 season: the Football League programme was abandoned due to the outbreak of the Second World War. The West Ham side, which won 3-1, included goalkeeper Harry Medhurst, whose son Norman was to become the physiotherapist for the England national side and, eventually, Plymouth Argyle. Two months later, The Pilgrims entered the South West Regional League.

Plymouth took a pounding during the Second World War, with many parts of the city destroyed by enemy action. Devonport Naval Base was a clear target for German bombing and Home Park, just a couple of miles away, did not escape. The grandstand was completely destroyed during 1941, the seating being reduced to a pile of rubble at the bottom of a large crater, by high explosives and a huge fire. Official club records were lost in a blazing inferno, set off by incendiary bombs and fed on furniture which local residents had stored in the stand for safe keeping during the raids. As a result of the attack, one of the most picturesque stands in the League was ruined. No other club suffered such extensive damage. Troops that had returned from Dunkirk made their camp behind the Barn Park end of the stadium and, in order to screen air defences, smoke generators were placed in the car park behind the Devonport End. Meanwhile, in the area behind the site of the grandstand, members of the US Navy constructed a warehouse. The Americans made good use of what was left of the Home Park playing surface by organising baseball matches.

ALL COMMUNICATIONS TO BE ADDRESSED TO THE SECRETARY

TELEPHONE 71933.   TELEGRAMS: TRESADERN, ARGYLE, PLYMOUTH

Plymouth Argyle Football Co., Ltd.

SECRETARY-MANAGER
CAPT. J. TRESADERN

Private Address :
   GREEN GABLES,
   GREAT BERRY ROAD,
   CROWNHILL, PLYMOUTH.

HOME PARK,
PLYMOUTH.

.... 194......

I am endeavouring to get hold of about a dozen weeding forks and some hoes to chop down the terrace weeds. There is also the question of tidying up the rubble on the old stand site so that we will look ship-shape when the season starts.

By the way we open the season at Southampton on Aug 25th and Southampton at Home Park on Sept. 1st

The dressing rooms are beginning to look habitable once again inside and when we get the hot water system installed, the players quarters will be quite comfortable with a bath room for each team.

Kind regards.

Yours truly,
J Tresadern.

One of the letters written by manager Jack Tresadern during the summer of 1945 appealing for practical help to clear the weeds on the Home Park terraces. Note that the headed paper included Mr Tresadern's private address!

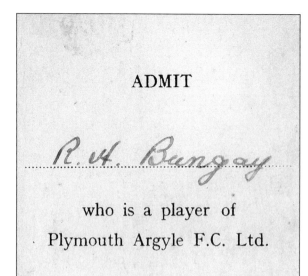

ADMIT

R. H. Bungay

who is a player of
Plymouth Argyle F.C. Ltd.

J. Tresadern,
Secretary-Manager.

Reg Bungay, whose season ticket from 1934/35 you have already seen, returned to represent the club during the 1944/45 season in the Plymouth and District League, The Plymouth Combination League and the Devon Senior Cup. The following season, although he did not play in the Football League South campaign, he did make two appearances in the Football League War Cup. The player's pass was personally issued by the secretary-manager Jack Tresadern.

Sir Clifford Tozer J.P., who, with the new Board of Directors, dedicated himself to the enormous task of rebuilding the club and Home Park. Tons of rubble from the ruins of the city centre were dumped in the craters and on the banking around the pitch. The wrecked stand was cleared and temporary seating installed in its place. A makeshift boardroom was erected and obsolete tramcars became the official club offices. On matchdays, a double-decker bus was driven alongside the touchline to serve as dressing rooms on the lower deck and directors' and press boxes on top.

Six

Peace and Promotion

Following the declaration of peace, The Pilgrims were able to compete in the Football League South for the 1945/46 season. Then it was back to Division Two action and, as this picture shows, it was all smiles as the staff return for duties on 29 July 1946 – despite the devastated Mayflower Terrace in the background. From left to right, standing: Archie Gorman (Reserve Team Trainer), Tommy Briggs, Alf Miller, Harry Butler, Bob Royston, Bill Strauss, Billy Hurst, Syd Rawlings, Alec Dyer, Alec Govan, George Poyser, Lou Tinkler, Len Boyd, Bill Shortt, Tommy Parnaby, Dave Thomas, George Silk, Ellis Stuttard, Reg Gibson, Len Jones, Alec Holland, Stan Dixon, Syd Rundle, Bill Harper (First Team Trainer). The kneeling man is Paddy Brown.

Forward Ernie Edds made his Argyle debut in the 2-1 defeat at Spurs on 23 November 1946. The occasion was recorded by local cartoonist Percy N. Dollery.

A week later, The Pilgrims beat Swansea Town by an identical score. The reference in another Dollery masterpiece 'The Swans' Attire' leads you to the colour of their kit – all white.

Plymouth Argyle, F.L. Div. II. Season 1946-7

Date	Opponents	Gnd.	Result 1946—47 For	Agst.	Date	Opponents	Gnd.	Result 1946—47 For	Agst.
1946					**1947**				
Aug. 31	West Ham Utd. ...	H	3	1	Jan. 1	Chesterfield ...	A	1	4
Sept. 2	Millwall ..	A	1	1	,, 4	Sheffield Wed. ..	H	4	
,, 7	Sheffield Wed. ..	A	1	2	,, 11	(F.A. Cup) ..		0	
,, 11	Chesterfield ..	H	0	2	,, 18	Fulham ...	A	3	1
,, 14	Fulham ..	H	2	3	,, 25	Bury ...	H		
,, 21	Bury	A	3		Feb. 1	Luton Town ...	A	4	3
,, 28	Luton ...	H	2	1	,, 8	Coventry City ..	A	0	3
					,, 15	Leicester City ..	H	2	0
Oct. 5	Coventry City ..	H	2	2	,, 22	Notts. Forest ...	A	2	3
,, 12	Leicester City ..	A	2	4					
,, 19	Notts. Forest ..	H	2	0	March 1	Southampton ..	H	2	3
,, 26	Southampton ..	A	1	5	,, 8	Newport County	A	5	1
					,, 15	Barnsley ..	H	1	2
Nov. 2	Newport County	H	4	1	,, 22	Burnley ..	A		2
,, 9	Barnsley ..	A	3	1	,, 29	Tottenham H. ..	H	3	4
,, 16	Burnley ..	H	2	2					
,, 23	Tottenham H. ..	A			April 4		H		
,, 30	Swansea Town	H	2		,, 5	Swansea Town ..	A	2	
					,, 7	Bradford	H	1	
Dec. 7	Newcastle Utd.	A	2	3	,, 8	Bradford ..	A	0	2
,, 14	West Brom. A. ..	H	2	6	,, 12	Newcastle Utd. ..	H	5	
,, 21	Birmingham City	A	3	4	,, 19	West Brom. A. ...	A		
,, 25	Manchester City	A	3		,, 26	Birmingham C. ...	H	0	
,, 26	Manchester City	H	3		May 3	Millwall	H	0	2
,, 28	West Ham Utd.	A	1	4					

Kick-Off Times		Kick-Off Times	
Aug., Sept., Oct.	3.15 p.m.	Nov. 26 to Jan. 15	2.30 p.m.
Nov. 1 to Nov. 14	3 p.m.	Jan. 16 to Jan 31	3 p.m.
Nov. 15 to Nov. 24	2.45 p.m.	Feb. to May	3.15 p.m.

The fixture card, duly completed with League results from the 1946/47 season. Note the staggered kick-off times indicated at the foot of the card.

PLYMOUTH ARGYLE SUPPORTERS' CLUB

MOTOR COACH EXCURSION

to

SOUTHAMPTON

SATURDAY, OCTOBER 26th, 1946

Depart Princess Square 6 a.m. sharp

Member's Name ....

Coach No. .... Seat ....

W. E. Jutson, *Hon. Sec.*

An unused excursion ticket for a game at Southampton in the 1946/47 season.

A glorious aerial shot of Home Park on 10 January 1948, as over 36,000 spectators watch the FA Cup match against Luton Town. The only covered accommodation is at The Devonport End. It is evident, by looking just beyond the ground, that not many supporters travelled to the match by car.

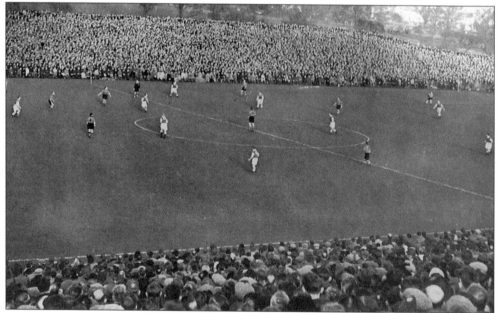

Home Park was packed with 40,000 spectators for the visit of Wolves on 7 January 1950 in the Third Round of the FA Cup. A 1-1 draw took the sides back to Molineux, where The Pilgrims suffered a 3-0 defeat. England captain Billy Wright was just one of a number of internationals who beat Argyle 2-1 when the two sides met again in the Third Round on 6 January 1951, in which season Wolves progressed to the Semi-finals.

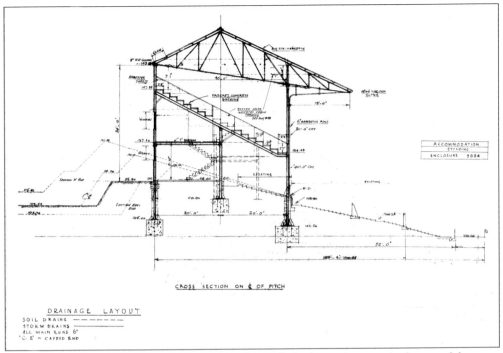

The side elevation of the new grandstand, in front of which can be seen the layout of the steps on the Mayflower Terrace.

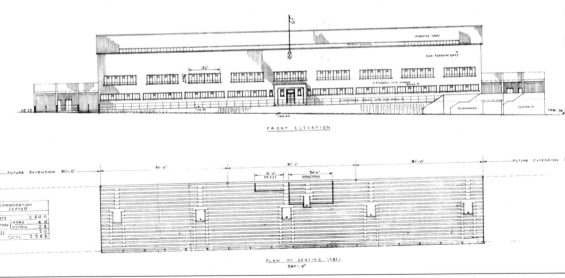

Dated 8 May 1951, this is the final plan of the front elevation of the new grandstand, designed by Archibald Leitch. He was at the forefront of many such structures, including those at Tottenham and Glasgow Rangers. The Home Park project was the last of the type ever built. Originally seating 2,500 supporters, a sixty-eight seat directors' box and a press area for twenty reporters, there have since been alterations. Extensions to the stands have been added, as well as a hospitality area to the rear of the structure. The press box is now found in an enclosed section at the top of the seating area.

Under Jimmy Rae, Plymouth Argyle clinched the Division Three (South) title at the conclusion of the 1951/52 season, finishing five points ahead of Reading. Of the twenty-three League matches played at Home Park, there were nineteen wins with just one defeat. This picture of the team comes complete with signatures (although Neil Dougall's – on his shorts – has faded somewhat). From left to right, back row: Neil Dougall, Pat Jones, Bill Shortt, Jack Chisholm, Paddy Ratcliffe, John Porteous. Front row: Gordon Astall, George Dews, Maurice Tadman, Peter Rattray, Alex Govan.

The Division Three (South) Championship trophy was carried through the centre of Plymouth in an open top coach, immediately after the team arrived home from the last game of the season at Norwich. After stepping off the train at North Road station, an estimated 70,000 people cheered along the route to the reception at The Grand Hotel. Note that the post Second World War reconstruction still taking place in New George Street as the motor coach progresses slowly through.

'Jumbo' Jack Chisholm, the gentle giant who led the team to promotion glory, meets the city's Lord Mayor at a civic reception.

The promotion team could not be accused of being all at sea – but one group of avid fans certainly were. All the crew of *HMS Bermuda* signed this celebratory post card, some of who were depicted, along with the 'Devon Belle', sitting proudly upon a promotion table.

Seven

Up, Down and Abroad

The visit to Doncaster on 18 April 1953 resulted in a 1-1 draw, helping The Greens to equal their previous best-ever position of fourth in Division Two. Bill Shortt climbs to grasp the ball from Rovers' centre forward, R.W. Harrison.

PLYMOUTH ARGYLE FOOTBALL CLUB

JUBILEE BANQUET

CONTINENTAL HOTEL
PLYMOUTH

on

MONDAY, MAY 4, 1953

———

LIST OF GUESTS

A Jubilee banquet was held at the Continental Hotel on 4 May 1953. The guest list contained current and past players and management personnel, civic dignitaries, influential people from local commerce and sundry well-known figures with football connections.

Division Two action from 16 April 1954: a 2-2 draw against West Ham United at Upton Park. Bill Shortt dives to gather the ball, surrounded by defenders Arthur Morgan (3), 'Jumbo' Chisholm (5) and Paddy Ratcliffe (on the goal line).

A tour of the United States of America in the summer of 1954 brought an additional match to those scheduled in the official itinerary, when the Chicago League Champions side provided the opposition on 29 May. Of the ten games played, Argyle won eight, scoring forty-eight goals and conceding nineteen. Included in the sightseeing schedule was a visit to the Plymouth Motor Works at Detroit, and the Paramount Film Studios in Hollywood, where many big-screen stars of the day were introduced to the players.

PLYMOUTH ARGYLE FOOTBALL CLUB

TOUR

OF

UNITED STATES OF AMERICA

1954

LIST OF OFFICIALS AND PLAYERS:

Sir Clifford Tozer, J.P.	*Chairman*
Mr. E. S. Dobell	*Vice-Chairman*
Mr. W. J. R. Heath	*Director in Charge*
Mr. J. Rae	*Manager*
Mr. G. Taylor	*Trainer*

J. Chisholm (*Captain*)   N. Dougall (*Vice-Captain*)

L. Major, W. Shortt, P. Ratcliffe, P. Jones, G. Robertson, A. Morgan,
T. McShane, J. Porteous, J. Crawford, S. McCrory, N. Langman, E. Edds,
M. Davies

ITINERARY

Tuesday, 27th April		*Dep.* Southampton ss "Ile de France"
Monday, 3rd May		*Arr.* New York, Paramount Hotel
Tuesday, 4th May		*Dep.* New York
Wednesday, 5th May		*Arr.* Chicago, Atlantic Hotel
Friday, 7th May	0·4	*Match:* (Dortmund of Germany), Soldier Field Stadium
Saturday, 8th May		*Dep.* Chicago
Saturday, 8th May		*Arr.* St. Louis, Fairgrounds Hotel
Sunday, 9th May	8·4	*Match:* (St. Louis Simpkins), Public School Stadium
Tuesday, 11th May		*Dep.* St. Louis
Tuesday, 11th May		*Arr.* Denver, (Hotel notified later)
Thursday, 13th May		*Match:* (Colorado All Stars), Denver Bear Baseball Stadium
Friday, 14th May		*Dep.* Denver
Friday, 14th May		*Arr.* Los Angeles, Plaza Hotel, Hollywood
Sunday, 16th May		*Match:* (Dortmund of Germany), Wrigley Field
Thursday, 20th May		*Match:* (Los Angeles All Stars), Rancho La Cienega Stadium
Friday, 21st May		*Dep.* Los Angeles
Friday, 21st May		*Arr.* San Francisco (Hotel notified later)
Sunday, 23rd May		*Match:* (San Francisco All Stars), Ground notified later
Monday, 24th May		*Dep.* San Francisco
Monday, 24th May		*Arr.* Chicago, Atlantic Hotel
Tuesday, 25th May		*Match:* (Chicago All Stars), Shewbridge Stadium
Wednesday, 26th May		*Dep.* Chicago
Thursday, 27th May		*Arr.* Detroit, Fort Shelby Hotel
Sunday, 30th May		*Match:* (All Star Detroit)
Monday, 31st May		*Dep.* Detroit
Tuesday, 1st June		*Arr.* New York, Paramount Hotel
Wednesday, 2nd June		*Match:* (German American League) Eintracht Stadium)
Thursday, 3rd June		*Dep.* New York, ss "Flandre"
Wednesday, 9th June		*Arr.* Plymouth.

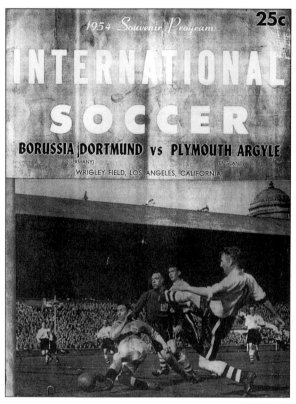

The opening match in Chicago against Borussia Dortmund resulted in a 4-0 defeat. For the fourth match of the tour, again against Dortmund, but played in Los Angeles, another defeat – this time 3-1. Here is the front cover and line-up page from the Wrigley Field match programme.

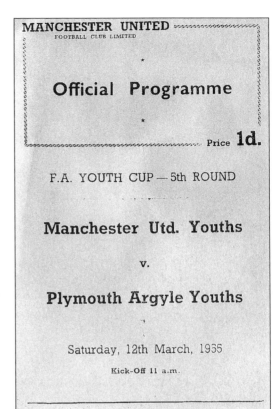

MANCHESTER UNITED
FOOTBALL CLUB LIMITED

*

Official Programme

*

Price **1d.**

F.A. YOUTH CUP — 5th ROUND

Manchester Utd. Youths

v.

Plymouth Argyle Youths

Saturday, 12th March, 1955

Kick-Off 11 a.m.

Stars of the future were on show in the FA Youth Cup Fifth Round tie between Manchester United and Plymouth Argyle on 12 March 1955. Included in the United side at No. 5 is Duncan Edwards, playing against an Argyle side for the only time in his short career. Dreams of a first team match against Manchester United were dealt a blow with relegation in 1956.

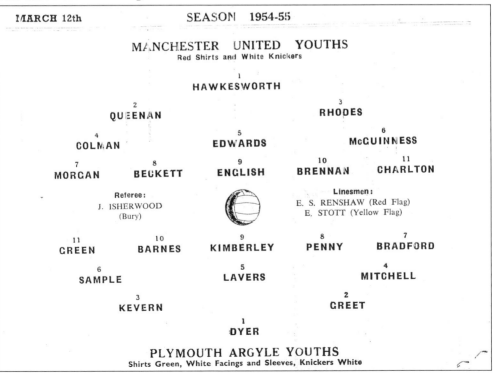

MARCH 12th   SEASON 1954-55

MANCHESTER UNITED YOUTHS
Red Shirts and White Knickers

1
HAWKESWORTH

2   3
QUEENAN   **RHODES**

4   5   6
COLMAN   **EDWARDS**   **McGUINNESS**

7   8   9   10   11
MORGAN   **BECKETT**   **ENGLISH**   **BRENNAN**   **CHARLTON**

Referee:
J. ISHERWOOD
(Bury)

Linesmen:
E. S. RENSHAW (Red Flag)
E. STOTT (Yellow Flag)

11   10   9   8   7
GREEN   **BARNES**   **KIMBERLEY**   **PENNY**   **BRADFORD**

6   5   4
SAMPLE   **LAVERS**   **MITCHELL**

3   2
KEVERN   **GREET**

1
DYER

PLYMOUTH ARGYLE YOUTHS
Shirts Green, White Facings and Sleeves, Knickers White

Telephone No. WESt Bromwich 0095.   Telegraphic Address: "Football, Westbromwich."

West Bromwich Albion Football Club, Ltd.

Winners First Division League Championship 1919-20.   Runners up 1924-25, 1953-54.
Winners Football Association Challenge Cup 1887-88, 1891-92, 1930-31, 1953-54.
                              Finalists 1885-86, 1886-87, 1894-95, 1911-12, 1934-35.
Winners Birmingham Cup 1885-86, 1893-94, 1894-95.
Winners Staffordshire Cup 1882-83, 1885-86, 1886-87, 1888-89, 1899-1900, 1901-2, 1902-3,
     1923-24, 1925-26, 1931-32, 1932-33, 1950-51.
Winners Midland Victory League Championship 1919.
Winners Midland Cup 1943-44.

Winners Football Association Charity Shield 1919-20.
Winners Birmingham Charity Cup 1899-1900, 1913-14, 1914-15, 1921-22
     1924-25.
Winners Second Division League Championship 1901-2, 1910-11,
                              Runners up 1930-31, 1948-49.
Winners B'ham District League Championship 1901-2, 1912-13, 1919-20.
Winners Central League Championship 1922-23, 1923-24, 1926-27, 1932-33,
     1933-34, 1934-35.

Secretary: Team Manager: Ground and
E. SMITH.   V. BUCKINGHAM   Registered Offices: "THE HAWTHORNS," WEST BROMWICH.

5th June, 1957.

Mr. A. H. Cole,
Plymouth Argyle Football Club Ltd.,
Home Park,
Plymouth.

Dear Mr. Cole,

        Thank you for your letter.   We are pleased to see
that you have signed our Player G. Barnsley and enclose, herewith,
form P.45 and Insurance Card.

        We have completed and forwarded the necessary forms to
the Football Association and Football League together with a
covering letter to explain the reason they have not been signed
by Mr. Smith personally.

        His League Service reads as follows:-

        Amateur   -   West Bromwich Albion 2/5/51.

        Professional -   "   "   "   2/12/52 to 4/6/57.

        We hope this Player will prove an acquisition to
your Club.

                        Yours sincerely,

                        Alan Love

                        Assistant Secretary.

Goalkeeper Geoff Barnsley spent six years with Division One side West Bromwich Albion, but made just one appearance. This letter confirming his transfer to Plymouth Argyle concludes with a note hoping he will prove to be a sound acquisition – indeed he was! Twenty games in his first season were followed by forty-one appearances in the Division Three Championship side.

This unusual shot shows just how popular football was with the public during the fifties, with hardly a space to spare on the terraces.

All smiles from the Argyle ball boys. Looking as smart as possible in their regulation track suits, with berets to complete the uniform. From left to right, back row: Michael Perry, Barry Fryer, Terry Avery, Michael Cole. Front row: Danny O'Reilly, Ian Clemens, Barry Blake, Russell Pearse.

In the first season following the disbanding of Divisions Three North and South, Plymouth Argyle became the first Division Three Champions in 1958/59, pipping Hull City by a single point. Attendances over 20,000 were commonplace as The Pilgrims lost just twice at Home Park. This team picture, taken early in the season, shows from left to right, back row: John L. Williams, George Robertson, David Downs, Johnny S. Williams, Jack Rowley (Manager), Geoff Barnsley, Reg Wyatt, Tommy Barrett, Neil Dougall, Ron Blindell (Chairman). Front row: Peter Anderson, Jimmy Gauld, Wilf Carter, George Baker, Harry Penk.

Eight
Happy Times in the Second Division

Argyle's promotion to Division Two saw regular attendances of over 25,000. The fans attending this match are packed in shoulder to shoulder in front of a sold-out grandstand, with an equally congested Devonport End in the background.

For supporters who wished to see their heroes playing away from home, the best source of information concerning the Supporters' Club travel arrangements were included in printed sheets. Note, at the top of the sheet, the reason why advertising could not be contemplated.

Dundee-born Jimmy McAnearney joined Plymouth Argyle from Sheffield Wednesday in 1960, along with George Kirby. In 135 League games for The Pilgrims, McAnearney hit the net on thirty-four occasions.

The "Green & Black" Club and Pool

PLYMOUTH

*Registered with the Commissioners of Customs and Excise,
also Plymouth City Council.*

RULES

1. Membership of the Club is open to all persons over the age of 21. Members pay 6d. to join the Club, and are asked to make a weekly voluntary donation of 2d. The income of the Club is used to assist the Plymouth Argyle Football Club.

2. Membership of the Club is not a condition of entry in the Pool, which is not restricted to members only.

3. Cash Only—All Pool transactions are on a cash basis. Clients must pay 10d. for each forecast made. No person under 21 years of age may participate in the Pool.

4. Clients are invited to forecast the numbers of three teams on the list to qualify for a dividend. Acceptance of coupons will be determined by the time of delivery to the Joint Secretaries, and all coupons must be received by 2.30 p.m. on the Saturday of each week. These should therefore be in the hands of the Agent by not later than Friday of each week.

5. Division of Pool—Winners will be paid the total amount staked on the Pool, subject to the right to deduct Pool Betting Duty and the necessary expenses.

Three Dividends will be paid:—

45 per cent among forecasts for 3 teams with the highest combined score.

30 per cent among forecasts for 3 teams with the second highest combined score.

25 per cent among forecasts for 3 teams with the third highest combined score.

6. Football Results will be taken from the Joint Secretaries' copy of the *Western Evening Herald* (Football edition) and *Western Independent* and payment of dividends will be made only from these records.

7. Postponed matches—Where any team does not play as printed the result counted shall be that of the next playing team below it on the list of teams, e.g. if No. 6 does not play it takes the result of No. 7 and so on. If the last numbered team does not play it takes the result of No. 1 or the next playing team below that. Abandoned matches the result at the end of play counts. Extra time does not count.

8. The decision of the Committee of the Green and Black Club shall be final and binding in all cases.

9. All business must be transacted through the Agent from whom the coupons are received.

POOL HEADQUARTERS
134 Desborough Road, St. Jude's, Plymouth.
(Telephone: 65280.)

Printed by Hitchings & Mason, 54 Well Street, Plymouth. Phone 65801.

Many fans subscribed to the 'Green and Black' club, raising valuable funds for Argyle. The rule sheet describes how the scheme was operated. During the summer of 1961, the efforts of those who ran the 'Green and Black' were rewarded, with the Supporters' Club able to clear the Argyle bank overdraft.

When local newspapers provided the only publicity outlet for forthcoming matches, posters were a regular sight around the city to advertise games at Home Park. Each month, three hundred were printed and distributed, detailing all first and reserve team games.

Reserve team football played in the Football Combination League enabled fans to see well-known names from both sides in each encounter, as illustrated by this single sheet programme from two of the strongest sides in the early 1960s – West Ham United and Argyle.

WEST HAM UNITED F.C.

BOLEYN GROUND, GREEN STREET, UPTON PARK, LONDON, E.1

Directors: R. H. PRATT, J.P. (Chairman)
L. C. CEARNS (Vice-Chairman)   W. F. CEARNS   R. G. BRANDON
Manager: R. GREENWOOD   Secretary: E. CHAPMAN
Honorary Consultant: W. ALEXANDER LAW, Esq., O.B.E., M.D., F.R.C.S.
Medical Officer: DR. J. C. BELL, M.B., Ch.B

PLYMOUTH ARGYLE Reserves

FOOTBALL COMBINATION

SATURDAY 6th JANUARY 1962 at 2.30 p.m.

OFFICIAL PROGRAMME   No. 34   ONE PENNY

WEST HAM UNITED Res.	PLYMOUTH ARGYLE Res.
Colours: Claret Jerseys, Light Blue Sleeves, White Shorts	Colours: Green Shirts, Black Facings White Shorts
1 Brian Rhodes	1 John Leiper
2 Eddie Presland	2 Dave Roberts
3 Jack Burkett	3 Richard Davis
4 Eddie Bovington	4 Mike Reeves
5 Bill Lansdowne	5 Reg Wyatt
6 Martin Peters	6 Len Casey
7 Derek Woodley	7 Stuart Brace
8 Ron Boyce	8 John Brown
9 Alan Sealey	9 Alex Gordon
10 Ron Brett	10 Keith Williams
11 Brian Dear	11 Adrian Thorne

Referee: Mr. J. H. ROBINSON (London, S.W.1)
Linesmen: Red Flag: : Mr. R. A. PAINE (Southall, Middlesex)
Yellow Flag: Mr. R. J. BANISTER (Worthington, Sussex)

Can I have your autograph? Argyle's Dave Corbett (right) with plenty of pen work ahead of him, together with Colin Dobson, on the occasion of being selected as a substitute for the England under-23s' clash against Belgium at Home Park in 1962.

The Pilgrims finished in a creditable fifth position in Division Two at the end of the 1961/62 season, ending it under the leadership of Ellis Stuttard. The final match of the campaign brought Liverpool, who were already assured of the Division Two Championship, to Home Park. The home side led the congratulations to the visitors as they took to the field, with future Pilgrim Jim Furnell donning the Liverpool goalkeeper's jersey behind skipper Ron Yeats.

The legendary Stanley Matthews in action at Home Park, taking on Argyle full-back Richard Davis on 23 March 1963.

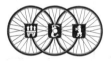

RUDE PRAVO • Trybuna Ludu • NEUES DEUTSCHLAND

Warszawa - Stadion X-lecia • 16. V. 63, godz. 14³⁰

ZAKOŃCZENIE VII ETAPU

XVI WYŚCIGU POKOJU

PRAHA - WARSZAWA - BERLIN

w programie:

MIĘDZYNARODOWE SPOTKANIE W PIŁCE NOŻNEJ

PLYMOUTHARGYLE FOOTBALL CLUB - LEGIA
(ANGLIA)   W.K.S.

ZAWODY HOKEJA NA TRAWIE **DANIA - POLSKA**

Zakończenie Małego Wyścigu Pokoju • 3 lotne finisze na stadionie • Zakończenie VII etapu • Dekoracja zwycięzcy etapu

Bilety łącznie z dod. na PKOI 25 zł, 20 zł i 15 zł, ulgowe dla młodzieży szkolnej i szeregowych W. P. 10 zł. Przedsprzedaż biletów na zam. zbiorowe w pawilonie Administ. Stadionu X-lecia.
Sprzedaż indywidualna w Orbisie ul. Bracka 16, SPATIF Al. Jerozolimskie 25 i PPUWT „Wisła" Al. Jerozolimska 2B. Sprzedaż biletów w dniu imprezy w kasach przy stadionie. Wymiana biletów bezpłatnych na leg. czł. i służbowe
GKKFiT odbywać się będzie w GKKFiT ul. Litewska 2B dla Zasłużonych Działaczy KF i Zasłużonych Mistrzów Sportu w pawilonie administracyjnym Stadionu Dziesięciolecia

On invitation from the Polish authorities, as part of a sporting festival, a tour of Eastern Europe kicked off on 16 May 1963 with a match against Legia Warsaw. This poster, rescued from the stadium, advertised the match as a secondary attraction to an international cycle race that passed through the arena – hence the spectacular attendance of 100,000.

Phase one of the terracing is complete on the Popular Side, still an uncovered area of the stadium.

The new roof over the Popular Side terracing ensured that the stadium boasted covering for as many as 25,000 spectators. The work was completed in 1964, during the Diamond Jubilee season. With the frame in place, Frank Lord celebrates a goal.

Meanwhile, the supporters get accustomed to the new surroundings.

The first overhead photo of Home Park showing the new roof, with part of the old Plymouth Zoo visible at the top of the picture.

After playing in every game for Swindon Town during 1962/63, finishing with promotion as runners-up to Northampton Town, Cliff Jackson joined The Pilgrims. The former England schoolboy international gained further attention by playing in the side that reached the League Cup Semi-finals in his second season at Home Park. After leaving Plymouth, he tasted further promotion with Crystal Palace, when they were elevated to Division One.

Seen from ground level, the Popular Side is again close to capacity as Cliff Jackson looks for the ball against Swindon Town

Making a guest appearance from the zoo, Clyde the llama takes a close look at the poster advertising Grandstand Bingo at Home Park. Held during the summer months on Wednesday evenings and Saturday afternoons, the shilling membership fee and weekly income provided funds for the Plymouth Argyle Development Association.

Malcolm Allison took charge of Plymouth Argyle's team affairs for the first time during the summer of 1964. Here is 'Big Mal' being welcomed to the club by his predecessor, caretaker-manager Andy Beattie, who had steered The Pilgrims to Second Division safety – although only by goal difference – the previous season.

Stars of the future! Norman Piper and Richard Reynolds proudly display their England youth international caps. Between them, they amassed over 340 appearances for Argyle. Piper was also selected for the FA Representative side and won four Under-23 caps before a transfer to Portsmouth, where he made 300 League outings. He then emigrated to America, to play his part in the growth of the game across the pond.

Reynolds made his first team debut in the League Cup Semi-final as a sixteen-year-old, exemplifying Malcolm Allison's philosophy of 'if they are good enough – they are old enough'. Like Piper, when Reynolds left The Greens, it was to move along the coast to Pompey.

Despite a keen eye for teenage talent, Allison made one particular signing that caused a stir: a twenty-eight year old bricklayer from Southern League side Bath City. However, the acquisition of Tony Book was an astute one. He missed just three games in two seasons at Home Park before Allison, by this time at Manchester City with Joe Mercer, once again signed the dependable right full-back, who picked up medals from League Championship, FA Cup, League Cup and Cup Winners' Cup successes and was also voted joint Footballer of the Year.

PLYMOUTH ARGYLE F.C.
HOME PARK, PLYMOUTH

The Football League Cup
Semi-Final
2nd Leg

versus

LEICESTER CITY
WEDNESDAY
FEBRUARY 10th
Kick-off 7.30 p.m.

GRAND STAND
TICKET

10/-

ROW   SEAT

Q   *21*

TO BE RETAINED
**PLEASE OCCUPY YOUR
SEAT EARLY**

Plymouth Argyle were just ninety minutes from the Final of the Football League Cup on 10 February 1965, after a narrow 2-3 defeat against Leicester City at Filbert Street in the first leg, with goals from Jon Williams and Mike Trebilcock. Alas, City scored the only goal of the second leg.

Barrie Jones arrived at Home Park from Swansea Town in September 1964 for a club-record fee of £45,000 (which was also a British record fee paid for a winger). Malcolm Allison's acquisition of Jones brought the rare occurrence of a current international playing for the club, although only one of his fifteen caps was acquired during his Pilgrim days. Jones made ninety-eight appearances for Argyle before being transferred to Cardiff City, in March 1967, for £20,000.

The playing strip of green, with a white and black band, was introduced to be 'worn when required'. Proudly showing their new colours are, from left to right, back row: Duncan Neale, Mike Reeves, Cliff Jackson, John Leiper, Noel Dwyer, Doug Baird, Richard Reynolds, Mike Trebilcock. Front row: Barrie Jones, Nicky Jennings, Tony Book, Derek Ufton (Manager), Johnny Newman, Johnny Williams, Frank Lord, George Taylor (Trainer).

Johnny Williams, who made his 400th League appearance on 23 October 1965 against Coventry City. Williams was a regular in the side for eleven seasons, but potential buyers were put off by Argyle's high regard for the midfielder-cum-half back, which was reflected in his monetary valuation.

Mike Bickle joined Argyle in December 1965 after amazing scoring feats with Co-op Welfare in the Devon Wednesday League and St Austell in the South Western League. His talents saw him give up his job as a milkman to score seventy-one goals in 181 League appearances, topping the club scoring charts for four consecutive seasons.

Johnny Newman became the first recipient of the Plymouth Argyle Player of the Year trophy. Here he is, receiving the award from the donor, Edgar Rickard.

Newman only scored nine goals in 298 matches – here's one of them: a penalty, successfully converted against Middlesbrough.

The day the World Cup came to Plymouth, 21 September 1966. The occasion was the Football League *v* Irish League match, the first-ever inter-league encounter held at Home Park. The Football League won 12-0 and Argyle's Johnny Newman was a substitute for the 'home' side, the starting eleven of which feature in this photograph. From left to right, back row: Peter Bonetti, Martin Peters, George Cohen, Bobby Moore, Jack Charlton, Ray Wilson. Front row: Terry Paine, George Eastham, Geoff Hurst, John Connelly, Johnny Byrne.

Bobby Moore displays the Jules Rimet Trophy to the city's Lord Mayor, Alderman T.H.L. Stanbury, at a civic reception following the game.

Two examples of fine local talent. John Tedesco (left) and Steve Davey signed professional terms on completing their apprenticeships. Davey became a folk hero, scoring forty-seven goals before adding to the list of former Pilgrims employed by Portsmouth.

Up for the Cup! A happy band of supporters, some with duffle bags and duffle coats, pictured outside Nottingham Forest's stadium ahead of the FA Cup Third Round encounter on 28 January 1967. The smiles had disappeared by the end of the afternoon as the First Division side recorded a 2-1 win.

The pre-season friendly against Stoke City on 3 August 1968. England goalkeeper Gordon Banks shows his safe handling in the City rearguard.

Bobby Saxton joined The Pilgrims from Derby County in February 1968 for £12,000 and was worth every penny! His strong defending would help Argyle to the Semi-final of the League Cup in 1973/74, and his return to Home Park in 1979 saw him take over the managerial hot seat.

Nine
Folk Heroes

When Billy Bingham took over at the helm from Derek Ufton, relegation to Division Three could not be avoided. It would be six years before Argyle were back in Division Two. Bingham was later allowed to combine his duties at Home Park with the position of team manager for Northern Ireland.

The team was not without players whose class stood out. Colin Sullivan would, in future years, be sold to Norwich City for a club record fee. Here, the young Sullivan climbs highest in the 2-1 defeat against Torquay United, with Danny Trainor and Bobby Saxton closing in. The Torquay defender is Ken Brown, who managed The Pilgrims in the late 1980s.

A family affair that was to the benefit of the club. Mr Tom Hefferson, with his sons Michael, Paul and Brian, set about another afternoon of selling Golden Goal tickets.

Action from 12 April 1969 and Mike Bickle (hand raised in anticipation) scores the first of his two goals in the 2-2 draw against Stockport County. Two weeks later, Argyle finished fifth in Division Three – fifteen points short of an immediate return to Division Two.

Dave Burnside once won a *Sunday Despatch* ball-juggling competition with 495 consecutive headers. He was also useful with his feet (which were invariably beneath rolled-down socks). In this photograph he has rounded the goalkeeper and is about to add to his tally in a match against Reading.

Home Park was chosen as the venue for the Under-23 international between England and Bulgaria on 8 April 1970. It was made even more memorable for Argyle fans when Sir Alf Ramsey announced he was to give the club's Norman Piper his first cap. England won 4-1 with goals by Roger Morgan (2), Tony Currie and David Nish – Mihailov replying for the visitors. A crowd of 28,056 were thrilled to see the star-studded line up of: Peter Shilton (Leicester City), Wilf Smith (Sheffield Wednesday), Derek Parkin (Wolves), David Nish (Leicester City), Martin Dobson (Burnley), Emlyn Hughes (Liverpool), David Thomas (Burnley), Norman Piper (Argyle), Keith Dyson (Newcastle United), Tony Currie (Sheffield United), Willie Morgan (Spurs), and substitutes Peter Mellor (Burnley), Paul Edwards (Manchester United) and Chris Garland (Bristol City). The picture shows the Argyle secretary, Graham Little, welcoming Ramsey and his players to the stadium.

Derek Rickard played in only the second half of the 1969/70 season, after giving up his employment with Devonport Dockyard. His nine League goals and general contribution to the team made him an instant favourite and his efforts were rewarded with the Player of the Year award.

One familiar landmark that has recently disappeared from inside Home Park is the Pilgrims' Shop. In this photograph, taken early in 1971, manager Ellis Stuttard and chief coach Bryan Edwards pose for a publicity shot.

How did he do that? Hughie Reed, the smallest man in the Argyle side, lets fly with a spectacular header from the edge of the Devonport End penalty area for the third goal in the 3-1 win over Torquay United on 27 December 1971.

No one could deny that the opponents selected for Bill Harper's testimonial match, in 1972, were appropriate, as Argyle faced the mighty Arsenal. Bill had joined The Pilgrims from The Gunners in December 1932 and served the club not only as a player, but also coach, groundsman, kit man, laundryman and in many more unofficial roles. He remained a supporter of Plymouth Argyle right up to his passing in April 1989 at the age of ninety-two, but his name will always be remembered through Harper's Park, the training ground adjoining the main stadium complex. During his testimonial year, Bill received one of the latest televisions available, made by the Bush company.

Here's to 1973! Manager Tony Waiters is flanked by the players wearing the appropriate numbers: Jim Furnell (1), Jimmy Hinch (9), Keith Allen (7) and Dave Provan (3).

A month later, the side had progressed to the Fourth Round of the FA Cup and a draw against Leeds United at Elland Road. There was anything but disgrace in the 2-1 defeat. Leeds goalkeeper David Harvey faces an anxious moment as Argyle mount an attack. United progressed to the Final, only to be beaten by Sunderland.

The night Pele played in Plymouth. Santos, on a European tour, made Home Park one of their ports of call. Little did the packed audience know that Santos were holding Argyle to ransom for extra money before the delayed kick-off. On seeing the level of interest that their presence had created, a demand of £2,500 more than the agreed fee was made by the visitors. Club chairman, Robert Daniel, could not inform the crowd of over 37,000 that the match would have to be called off – with the Brazilians sat in their dressing room refusing to get changed – so there was no alternative but to give in to the demand (whilst making clear his feelings towards the act). Smiles returned after the match, as Pele posed for this picture with Alan Welsh, Johnny Hore, Colin Sullivan and Jim Furnell. Argyle had won 3-2, thanks to goals from Mike Dowling (one of the fiercest shots ever seen at Home Park), Derek Rickard and Jimmy Hinch. Pele left his mark on the match with a successful penalty kick. The cash was handed over at the Holiday Inn, following a post-match reception. Santos officials were informed that they would be reported to the Football Association with the threat of requesting a ban on future matches in England. 'Plenty more countries' came the reply. Supporters learned of the behind-the-scenes mayhem the following day.

Full-back John Hore, who joined The Pilgrims as an apprentice in 1962, was a tower of strength in the promotion side of 1975, fittingly in his testimonial year. The Cornishman was to later return to Argyle as manager and lead the side to the FA Cup Semi-finals.

Ten
The Magic of Mariner

Paul Mariner joined Plymouth Argyle on his twentieth birthday from non-League Chorley Town and became an instant favourite at Home Park. His twenty goals during the 1974/75 season, in a phenomenal partnership with Billy Rafferty, were an integral part of the promotion campaign. In October 1976, having scored fifty-six goals in 134 League games, Mariner was signed by Bobby Robson at Ipswich Town for a price of £220,000, a record fee for both clubs. His career blossomed with FA and UEFA Cup honours, thirty-five England caps and sixty appearances for Arsenal.

Home fans were still permitted to stand on the Barn Park terrace in the early parts of the 1970s and these youngsters show that they were two of the few who purchased the unpopular *Pilgrim* newspaper, which had replaced the traditional programme.

Plymouth has had more than its fair share of bad weather over the years and problems with drainage at Home Park did not help with match preparations. Head groundsman, Harry Elsworth, is seen here on a Saturday morning, working hard to prepare, as best he can, the Barn Park end of the pitch. He efforts were rewarded as the afternoon's match went ahead!

On the subject of the elements, here is a piece of the action from the League Cup Semi-final first leg against Manchester City on 23 January 1974. After defeating Burnley, Queen's Park Rangers and Birmingham City – all First Division sides and away from home – the reward was a place in the penultimate stage of the competition for the second time. Although played on a Wednesday afternoon, because of the power crisis, over 30,000 turned out to see the 1-1 draw which took place on a mud bath. Paul Mariner, Steve Davey and Ernie Machin are the Argyle men in view, with City's Colin Bell looking a little lost. Rodney Marsh can be seen looking on in the background.

Seen from the sky, Home Park has always been a grand sight, but note the strange circular object in the bottom left-hand corner. A big top was erected in the club car park to house the touring Royal Ballet. In stark contrast, singing sensations The Wurzels also appeared (but not on the same bill).

A leap above Mike Green and the ball belongs to Jim Furnell, with Alan Rogers in attendance, at Dean Court on 11 January 1975. It was the occasion of a huge win (7-3) and dreams of promotion were becoming a reality. The Bournemouth player is Neil Hague, who had joined The Cherries at the end of the previous season.

Bill Rafferty waits for the Hereford 'keeper to slip up at Edgar Street on 8 March 1975. He scored twice in the comfortable 5-1 away victory.

Jim Furnell makes a save on 29 March 1975 – but look at the Brighton & Hove Albion player: running in towards goal: it's none other than the former Argyle man Ernie Machin.

Defending a free kick against Port Vale on 19 April 1975: Phil Burrows, Hugh McAuley, John Delve, Brian Johnson, John Hore and Bill Rafferty. The 2-2 draw, watched by 22,447, secured a point towards the final position as runners-up in Division Three. The top deck of the building in view is now the location of the Chisholm Lounge.

Back in Division Two! As far as some supporters were concerned, the only gripe was the distinct lack of the traditional green in the new playing strip. From left to right, back row: Keith Blunt (Assistant Manager), John Hore, Neil Rioch, Jim Furnell, Dave Sutton, Milija Aleksic, Geoff Banton, George Foster, Tony Waiters (Manager). Middle row: Alan Brown (Chief Coach), Bobby Saxton, Alan Rogers, Barrie Vassallo, Mike Green, Bill Rafferty, Graeme Hurn, Phil Burrows, Mick Horswill, Tommy Eggleston (Physiotherapist). Front row: Ian Pearson, Hugh McAuley, Peter Darke, Colin Randell, John Delve, Paul Mariner, Brian Johnson, Chris Harrison, Peter Hardcastle.

The unsung heroes of Home Park. A fine body of men, affectionately known as Dad's Army, kept the stadium in shipshape fashion, working in all weathers. The intrepid chaps are pictured at an annual Christmas social, where turkeys were presented to players and staff members. From left to right, back row: Ron Prettyjohns, Alf Nicholson, Graham Little (Club Secretary), Harold Light, Jack Ferrand. Front row: Bill Mealing, Ron West, Claude Jones.

Argyle's return to Division Two saw many big names appear in opposition at Home Park. Paul Mariner scored the only goal against Nottingham Forest on 20 December, although in this shot his effort flew over the crossbar. Also in the picture is Mariner's striking partner, Billy Rafferty, along with the Forest goalkeeper, Peter Wells, and defenders Frank Clark and Ian Bowyer – who in future years was to become a coach at Home Park.

Paul Mariner and Chelsea goalkeeper Peter Bonetti take a breather in the 2-3 defeat on 11 September 1976, in front of 18,356 spectators who saw the Argyle striker add to his tally for the club.

Eleven

An Eventful Tenth Decade

The programme from the match that won promotion on 29 April 1986. The programme was dated 31 March, when the fixture was postponed because of a waterlogged pitch, but issued four weeks later with an explanatory insert.

(H) ALL FOR ARGYLE FUND

Nº 12992

Promoter: J. Furnell, 2 Jump Close, Roborough Green, Plymouth PL6 7AU

Grand Draw

1st PRIZE—COLOUR TELEVISION
2nd PRIZE—RADIO = 3rd PRIZE—(One year subscription Automobile Association plus Relay Breakdown Service)

Draw to take place August 24th before Argyle's First League Match versus Blackburn Rovers at Home Park.

Registered under Betting, Gaming and Lotteries Act 1963.   Cert. No. A951.

TICKET   10p

Money became a focal point for the running of the club as Brian Hall signed from Liverpool for a club record fee of £50,000, the majority of which was raised as a direct result of appeals to supporters. One such venture saw the '(H)all For Argyle' campaign, which included the sale of draw tickets.

The Argyle Lottery, brainchild of the commercial manager, Bill Pearce, set the standards for other football clubs to follow. Seen as essential towards the survival of the club, the lure of big-money weekly prizes, with each draw broadcast live on Plymouth Sound Radio, added to the excitement for supporters who took the chance to cash-in on the new initiative.

114

With Rafferty and Mariner no longer at Home Park, the slide down the Division Two table led to relegation in the summer of 1977. Tony Waiters was replaced by Mike Kelly, but his reign was a short one as the prospect of Division Four looked increasingly likely and Lennie Lawrence took over as acting manager. On 18 February, as if things were not bleak enough, the match against Bradford City saw The Pilgrims a goal down in blizzard conditions. The crowd of 2,843 – the lowest since the War – were invited to sit in the Mayflower Stand. They were relieved to see the match abandoned. The photo shows John Craven tackled by defender John Middleton.

A few days later, Malcolm Allison returned for a second stint in charge. Form improved and relegation in successive seasons was avoided, the campaign culminating in the 6-0 demolition of Bradford City (in the match previously postponed in a snowstorm).

The youth policy of the 1970s produced many fine young players. Goalkeeper Martin Hodge made his debut in 1978, but just over a year later began a much-travelled career when he joined Everton for £135,000.

Gary Megson was another young talent snapped up by the Merseyside club, with Argyle receiving a record fee of £250,000.

Fred Binney, although born in Plymouth, did not play for Argyle until the twilight years of his career. The 1978/79 season saw him claim twenty-six League goals, including the one that preceded this celebration against Swindon Town.

Lining up for the start of the 1980/81 campaign, which saw the side under the charge of former player Bobby Saxton climb to seventh in Division Three. From left to right, back row: Jeremy Collins, Mark Graves, Neil Hards, Forbes Phillipson-Masters, Geoff Crudgington, Chris Harrison, Brian Johnson. Middle row: Kevin Hodges, Colin Upton, Colin Randell, David Kemp, Donal Murphy, Leigh Cooper, Brian McNeill. Front row: John Uzzell, Brian Bason, John Peachey, George Foster, John Sims, Steve Morris, Tyrone James.

A fine sequence of photos showing David Kemp scoring a hat-trick against Carlisle United on 6 September 1980 – three of his twenty-four League goals in that season. In later years, he returned to Home Park as manager.

After completing his apprenticeship, defender John Uzzell loyally served the club for over twelve years, earning a testimonial during his lengthy (over 300 appearances) Home Park career. Here, we see the trusted left foot in action against Reading.

Following two years with Bobby Moncur as manager, John Hore took over the position. His main priority was to keep Argyle in Division Three, but the relegation battle was accompanied by a titanic run in the FA Cup. After succeeding against Southend, Barking, Newport County, Darlington and West Bromwich Albion, a win in the Quarter-final replay against Derby County sparked high spirits in the away dressing room at The Baseball Ground.

The man who broke thousands of hearts. The scorer of the goal that took Graham Taylor's Watford side to Wembley, George Reilly, is challenged by Chris Harrison.

The mass of fans that made the pilgrimage to Villa Park for the Semi-final against Watford. Impeccably behaved, outrageously noisy, yet appreciative after defeat.

To find a reliable goalkeeper, one needed to look no further than Geoff Grudgington during his nine years with The Greens. Brought to Home Park as a replacement for Martin Hodge, the former England schoolboy international was signed by Tommy Docherty at Aston Villa as a seventeen-year-old. However, it was at Crewe and Swansea, where he was an ever-present for four of his six seasons, that he built a reputation for safe handling. For seven years, he was the automatic choice for The Pilgrims, before being controversially replaced by Steve Cherry in a FA Cup tie at Highbury in 1987. His perfect attendance record in the FA Cup Semi-final run of 1983/84 and the promotion run, two years later, contributed to a total of 382 League and Cup games for Argyle (out of a career total of 732). 'Crudgie' was later appointed as reserve team manager and youth coach and awarded a testimonial. He was destined to go on to be a main contributor in the club's Cornish Centre of Excellence.

Leigh Cooper was another gem of the 1980s, having progressed through the club's youth policy. His League debut came two years after signing apprentice terms in 1977 and he proved as astute at full-back as he was when playing in midfield. When he was appointed club captain, at the young age of twenty-two, he took it ably in his stride. To lead Argyle to the FA Cup Semi-final was a great achievement, as was his invaluable contribution towards Argyle's recapture of a Division Two place. A long association with Truro City began when he signed as a player under Steve Massey and he went on to very successfully manage the Jewson South Western League side before looking for a new challenge in local football by becoming the manager of Saltash United in June 1998. Another player who enjoyed the benefits of a testimonial, Home Park would have been a poorer place if Leigh Cooper had not been discovered playing football in Reading by Argyle scout Micky Hill.

In 1984, this young man was seen as one for the future. An unassuming central defender, Adrian Burrows had previously served at Mansfield Town and Northampton Town. John Hore saw qualities in him and brought 'Shades' to Plymouth. After a spell out of the first team under Dave Smith, he managed to prove his character and command a regular starting place. The romance of football was on display for Adrian's testimonial – against Sheffield Wednesday, for whom his father Horace played when he won his three England caps in 1934 and 1935. Burrow's dependency was never questioned by the supporters or referees. It was therefore sad to see him sent off for the first time in his final game for Argyle, over a disputed handball in the play-off semi-final at Burnley in 1994, which ruled him out of the return leg.

In an amazing stint of loyalty, Kevin Hodges joined the club as an apprentice in 1976, and soon became a member of the South West and Wales Youth Cup winning side. Over the next seventeen years, he made a club record 541 League and sixty cup appearances, scoring eighty-three goals. In today's game, it is doubtful that such a record (which merited testimonials after ten and fifteen years) in the lower divisions will ever be repeated. With the FA Cup Semi-final appearance adding to his experience, not only did the Dorset-born player lead the scoring chart with sixteen in the 1985/86 promotion campaign, he was also presented with the Player of the Year Trophy to round off a perfect season in which he appeared in every game. Off the field, he quickly became known as a thoroughly decent chap – in all, the model professional. After leaving Argyle, he was appointed player-coach at Torquay United, but returned to Home Park in June 1998 to take charge of The Pilgrims.

The completion of executive boxes gave a new dimension to comfort. Fully furnished and carpeted, each split-level box gives a superb view of the pitch with the added bonus of meals and refreshments served before the match and at half-time.

Dave Smith's appointment led to Second Division status after his first full season in charge. The penultimate game saw a crushing 4-0 home victory over Bristol City. 20,000 delirious fans saw Tommy Tyan score twice, with Garry Nelson and Russell Coughlin also on target, which triggered celebrations that lasted well into the night. Taken during that memorable campaign, this picture shows Garry Nelson, John Clayton, Kevin Hodges and Steve Cooper demonstrating their appreciation of the home support.

124

As well as his on-field achievements, the self-confessed 'Ciderman' became famed for his thoughts in prose, printed in the matchday programme, and his communication skills. He personally welcomed supporters to Home Park from the touchline twenty minutes before kick-off and explained any changes to his team. Here's his squad in training at Harper's Park, led by Leigh Cooper, Russell Coughlin, Gordon Nisbet, Kevin Hodges, John Uzzell and Chris Harrison.

Behind every great manager is a reliable right-hand man. Smith was able to call upon the services of the experienced Martin Harvey, which meant that the Argyle team was in the hands of a two-man team with a wealth of experience in the game.

125

One of the most lethal strikers the lower divisions of the Football League has ever known, Tommy Tynan merited legendary status at Home Park. After spells at Sheffield Wednesday, Lincoln City and Newport County (where he formed a formidable partnership with John Aldridge), he joined Argyle under Bobby Moncur. But, in the summer of 1985, a move to Rotherham United for personal reasons gave Argyle fans good reason to assume that they had seen the last of him in a green shirt. However, towards the end of the next season he was back, albeit on loan, to seal the push for promotion. In the final nine games of the campaign he scored ten goals, including two against his parent club, after which Rotherham's manager, Norman Hunter, claimed that Dave Smith had broken an agreement not to play him in that match. Tynan then signed again on a permanent basis to take his full tally for the club to 126 goals in 262 League appearances. No wonder the fans sang 'There's only one Tommy Tynan'. In June 1998, Tynan returned to Home Park in the capacity of commercial manager.

Remember this great signing? Bobby Charlton was on duty for one night only, to take charge of a junior penalty shoot-out competition, and was welcomed to the club by Chairman Peter Bloom.

****** 1886-1986 ******

PLYMOUTH ARGYLE FOOTBALL CLUB

CENTENARY DINNER

HOLIDAY INN, PLYMOUTH

WEDNESDAY 29th OCTOBER 1986

The Centenary Dinner, held at The Holiday Inn, was attended by FA Chairman Bert Millichip and the Secretary of the Football League, Graham Kelly. Other speakers included Robert Hicks MP, Plymouth Argyle Chairman Peter Bloom, and Sam Rendell. A future President of the club, Sam spoke in his contemporary capacity as Vice-President. On-the-field success continued through the centenary season, with Tommy Tynan's eighteen goals helping to elevate The Pilgrims to a final position of seventh in Division Two by May 1987.

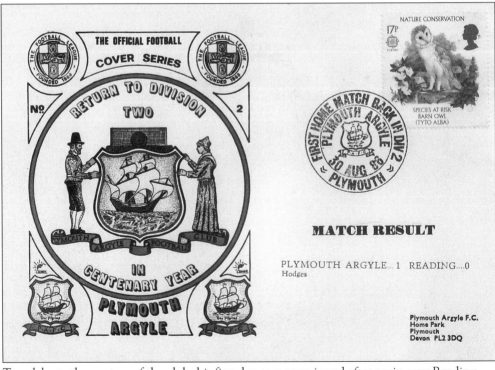

THE OFFICIAL FOOTBALL COVER SERIES

NO. 2

RETURN TO DIVISION TWO IN CENTENARY YEAR

PLYMOUTH ARGYLE

MATCH RESULT

PLYMOUTH ARGYLE... 1   READING....0
Hodges

Plymouth Argyle F.C.
Home Park
Plymouth
Devon PL2 3DQ

To celebrate the century of the club this first day cover was issued after a win over Reading.